CONGRESS AND CONSCIENCE

J. B. LIPPINCOTT COMPANY
PHILADELPHIA and NEW YORK

CONGRESS AND CONSCIENCE

Essays by

Congressman Jim Wright

Senator George McGovern

Senator Barry Goldwater

Congressman Charles E. Bennett

Congressman Albert H. Quie

Congressman John B. Anderson

JOHN B. ANDERSON, *editor*

☆ ☆ ☆ ☆ ☆ ☆ ☆ ☆

FOREWORD

With a few notable exceptions, practicing politicians are not prolific in their writing. It is not so much that they fear their inability to rise to the heights of a Caesar or a Churchill, for undue modesty is rarely an affliction suffered by those who enter the lists in pursuit of elective office. Rather it is that relentless and remorseless enemy of mankind, the swift passage of time, that prevents the politician from dispensing the same ineffable truths through the printed page as are poured forth from the political stump. He is generally so preoccupied with current events that he finds little time for his political testament until the scythe of time has severed him from his active political connections. Then in enforced retirement, he may be seized by the notion that he should become the great revealer of truth.

The essays in this book have all been written by men who are still active in the hurly-burly of American politics. It may, therefore, have a singular interest and attraction, we dare to presume, for those for whom politics, although a spectator sport, holds a cerebral as well as combative interest.

I am deeply grateful to my colleagues in the House and Senate who have collaborated with me in this writing project. I know that they have done so out of a conviction that this volume may help to shed some additional light on the political process peculiar to American democracy. I hope it may also indicate how principles of Christian morality affect the daily decisions of some of those who help mold and shape the institutions of that democracy. In addition, I am profoundly grateful to two young men who have served as Congressional staff aides.

Paul Henry, who left my Congressional staff to complete his doctoral studies at Duke University, assisted immeasurably in the early stages of the preparation of this volume. Without his initial encouragement it would have remained an abstraction.

Howard Moffett, who joined my staff later, has contributed untold zeal and imagination to the editorial supervision and organization of the material included in the pages that follow. In addition to countless suggestions for improvement in the content he has enjoyed the thankless task of riding herd on six busy Members of Congress who are oblivious to deadlines and have sometimes extended their Congressional immunity from correction and reproof beyond that which the Founding Fathers intended. Without their help the editor would have had an impossible task, and I gratefully acknowledge their indispensable assistance.

In addition, thanks are extended to the following other staff aides: Marshall Lynam of Congressman Jim Wright's staff; David Beale and Peter Stavrianos of Senator George McGovern's staff; Tony Smith from Senator Barry Goldwater's office; Richard Sewell of Congressman Charles Bennett's staff; and Keith Hall from the staff of Congressman Albert Quie.

John B. Anderson, M.C., Editor
Washington, D.C.

CONTENTS

INTRODUCTION

by Congressman
JOHN B. ANDERSON

Introduction
MAN'S NATURE AND GOD'S DESIGN
by the Honorable John B. Anderson

It is customary for busy men, when trespassing in print on
such a tender topic as Christian morality or such a weighty
one as the American political process, to offer profligate
apologies for their temerity, if not their talent. The rationale
for such apologies, of course, is that the depths of these subjects have been plumbed so sufficiently and so often that additional comment can only add confusion rather than enlightenment.

Cheerfully, we make bold to dispense with this time-
honored ritual, not because of any special talent for un-
covering and interpreting truth, but because our temerity is
dearly bought in an arena to which few are privy. For it is
in the halls of Congress, if anywhere, that the claims of
Christian morality and the exigencies of practical politics together leave their imprint on our national institutions and
our national life. The men who have contributed to this
volume have a unique perspective, as practicing Christian
politicians, on the hazards and hopes of trying to reconcile
the ethical ideals of the Judeo-Christian tradition with the
rough-and-tumble politics of the nation's capital.

The book has a double aspect as a result of the contributors' interests. On the one hand, the alert reader will quickly recognize that many of the questions posed in the essays are timeless. Each author, in his fashion, has been a seeker after truth which is in some sense lasting, in some sense immune from the corrupting influence of moths and dust. There is a timeless quality, for example, about the Dutch philosopher Spinoza's observation that no one should expect a government to act in accordance with the moral code that would be appropriate to the conduct of individuals; its problems are different. We may agree or disagree with the learned philosopher, but we recognize his problem as a valid one, and smile because it has yet to be solved.

On the other hand, it should be clear from the opening pages of the first essay that the treatment of these questions by the contributing authors is deeply influenced by the practical urgency of daily decisions and the countless minor conflicts of our particular calling. Perhaps no one has spelled out this dilemma quite so clearly as Abraham Lincoln, the great American President whose entire administration was colored by the anguish of trying to reconcile God's will with man's limitations:

I am approached with the most opposite opinions and advice, and that by religious men who are equally certain that they represent the divine will. I am sure that either the one or the other class is mistaken in that belief, and perhaps in some respects both. I hope it will not be irreverent for me to say that if it is probable that God would reveal his will to others on a point so connected with my duty, it might be supposed he would reveal it directly to me; for, unless I am more deceived in myself than I often am, it is my earnest desire to know the will of Providence in this matter. And if I can learn what it is, I will do it.

A word should be said about the structure of the book. It is really composed of six separate essays, each by an individual who has been concerned for some time with the subject he is writing about, and who has been left to develop the issue in his own terms and in his own style. The essays are open-ended. Nowhere is there any attempt to wring out of these six individuals a single, "correct" point of view, and readers will have plenty of opportunity to make up their own minds on the questions which recur throughout the volume. However, as we have worked on these essays, shared our thoughts, and tried to tie the many different ideas together in our own minds, several major themes became more and more clear, and a point first made in one essay found its echo as a leitmotiv in the next.

Perhaps the central problem posed throughout the book is the tension implicit in each chapter between God's expectations and man's capacities. This tension is suggested by the title of this introduction, "Man's Nature and God's Design," and we will speak of the attempt to reconcile the two in the business of politics, where men decide what kind of society they want to live in and what standards of behavior they expect of each other.

There are four great concepts—religion, ethics, law and politics—which find their way into the discussion at various points throughout the book. Each is unconscionably difficult to define and pin down, but it would perhaps be appropriate here to try to show how the four are related to each other and to the problems we will be discussing. Religion, ethics, law and politics are all ways—institutionalized in varying degrees—of attempting to influence how men behave toward each other and what kind of society they make with each other. But they come at the problem from quite different presuppositions, reflecting the tension we cited earlier between man's nature and God's design.

We can view the four concepts as elements in a spectrum. Religion is at one end of the spectrum, representing the revelation that God has made of his design for the universe and the conduct of human life. He has set values for man to live by, consonant with his plan for the whole of the created universe. Out of these values, which in the Christian tradition are revealed in the Bible, ethics grow. Ethics are rooted in the divine plan and in revealed religion, but they can be seen as an attempt to codify, for man in society, the rules and values which God has revealed in religion.

Politics approaches the problem of man's behavior in society from the opposite pole. Rather than the harmony of the divine plan, it begins with the experience of human conflict, which centuries of recorded history have documented beyond any doubt. This is the practical side of man's nature, which admits tacitly that man can never quite live up to the high ideals of God's design. Over the centuries, man has painfully developed procedures to deal with human conflict, to minimize it, to resolve it where possible, but above all not to let it destroy the society he wants to preserve; these procedures we call law.

This book, then, will attempt to shed a little perspective on each of these great concepts—religion, ethics, law and politics. It is easy enough to demonstrate the distinctions between them, but the reason for bringing them all together in one volume is that each is an attempt to write *values* into the conscious or unconscious behavior of men, and to influence the kind of society they try to achieve collectively. Men have always argued violently over each of these concepts, but at bottom they are always arguing over what kind of behavior they expect of each other and what kind of institutions they want to govern their lives. And the starting point for most of these discussions has always been either the ideal—as represented by morality, God's design, the "ought" of philosophy and ethics—or the practical, as represented by man's nature, the hard-knocks school of experience, the "is" against which so many arguments for an ideal order have foundered.

To this discussion, the Christian brings a distinctive point of view. For him, God has spoken on each of these points, and he sees a responsibility to bring his own vision of the good into line with God's design, to the extent that this is possible in a fallen world. Each of the essays reflects this concern in varying degrees, and it is the commitment of each of the writers represented here which may give this volume whatever value it has. Let us look for a moment at how the central themes are drawn out in the course of the six essays.

The first essay, by Congressman Jim Wright of Texas, plunges us right into the center of the dilemma by posing a question which, in different forms, will recur often in the succeeding chapters: Representative Wright asks, in effect, "If God does have a design that he wants implemented by fallible men, how are we to know what it is? Or more accurately, how can we be sure that we understand it more clearly than the next fellow?" Laced with a fair amount of wry Texas humor, Wright's essay makes a powerful case for humility and tolerance in the attempt to legislate our way to a better, more moral society. It sets the stage for a full consideration of the classic liberal and conservative positions on morality in politics, as interpreted by Senators George McGovern and Barry Goldwater.

In Senator McGovern's essay we have an able expression of the liberal Christian's view that institutional reform can and should be used to take some of the raw edge off the evil and injustice which we see around us. In "The Politics of Hunger," we see God's design thwarted in the operation of institutions geared to the limitations of human nature. The implicit argument is that widespread hunger in the world's best-fed society is a moral outrage, as offensive to the Creator as it is absurd to us. But when we try to attack this problem through our established political institutions—in this case the Congress and the executive branch—when we attempt to eliminate hunger and thus bring our society more in line with what we assume is God's design, we find ourselves stymied by what is euphemistically known as practical politics. We begin by asking, "What can we do to make ours a better society, where the food we have in overabundance gets to those who need it most as well as to those who never seem to lack for it?" And we bog down, somewhere along the way, in considering such questions as "Can we really do that without upsetting too many programs? Will it work? Can we expect men to behave that way?" Ultimately, human nature makes a mockery of God's design, which nevertheless lingers on to haunt our public life with its reminder of our own limitations.

Senator Barry Goldwater offers a clear exposition of the traditional conservative argument for individual responsibility rather than institutional reform. Where Senator McGovern clearly implies that God's design is thwarted by human nature in the operation of institutions, Senator Goldwater argues forcefully that, for better or worse, man's nature is part of God's design, and the personal limitations we try to overcome in improving our life together must cast doubt on our ability to identify God's will for the benefit of our fellowmen. The basic confusion stems from man's arrogant attempt to interpret God's will in terms of his own personal biases. Central to Senator Goldwater's argument is the thesis that society, in its institutional form, is neither moral nor immoral—individuals are. Thus if we really want to apply morality to politics, social problems, and the improvement of our society, we must personalize morality rather than try to institutionalize it. There is an inherent limit to the improvements that can be made in human society, for if God's design must be fulfilled by individual men, it will never be perfectly achieved due to the inherent weaknesses and limitations of human nature. We will find the themes running through these first three essays brought together in the final chapter, when we look at the way in which religious doctrine has influenced political ideology in America, and vice versa.

Senator Goldwater closes his essay with a discussion of the continuing controversy over Congressional ethics, which has grown more heated in every recent Congress. This takes us directly into a fuller discussion of personal standards of public morality by one of the House of Representatives' acknowledged experts on the subject, Representative Charles Bennett of Florida. Congressman Bennett argues that while we can never be completely successful in transforming the behavior of individual men, nevertheless within a given institution, in this case the Congress, we can try to make individuals more sensitive, and their behavior more responsive, to God's design—and by implication less subject to the caprice and weakness of man's nature. He holds out no hope of perfection, but argues that progress has been made and offers several concrete suggestions for further limiting opportunities for possible misconduct in the legislative branch.

Representative Albert Quie of Minnesota adds another perspective to the discussion of morality in politics, by tracing the history of relations between church and state in America. His essay presents the conflict between the divine will and human interests in the form of a potential conflict between the institutions which embody them. In terms of traditional Christian theology, he tells the story of how from the beginning of our society and culture we have tried to reconcile the conflicting claims of what Saint Augustine called the City of God and the City of Man. This question, central to the origins of American political and religious culture, leads us into a consideration of how the doctrine or ideology of the church has affected its view of its own role in society vis-à-vis the state. For it was in its role as a guardian of truth as well as in its role as a guardian of morality that the church first threatened to clash with the state in our history; in other words, political rights and political authority were often made contingent on a "correct" Christian theology in the early colonies, and the battle for authority that loomed so early was only tentatively resolved in the doctrine of the separation of church and state which was written into our Constitution. It is a tribute to the political genius of our Founding Fathers that they recognized and avoided this potential conflict insofar as they were able, by insuring that God's will and man's should each be given full and free expression, but separately, in church and civil state.

The book's final chapter is an attempt to disentangle the influence of religious doctrine on political expression in America, and vice versa, and to tie various other themes in the book together in the process. It begins with a discussion of the subtle and unofficial ways in which conservative theology has been linked to conservative politics, while liberal political persuasion seems to go hand in hand with a liberal theological expression. The essay attempts to trace the origins of the present alignment of interests first in the historic, turn-of-the-century debate between Fundamentalists and proponents of the Social Gospel, then in the earlier philosophical debate between political liberals and conservatives in the seventeenth and eighteenth centuries, and finally in the semantic confusion which resulted when New Deal liberalism took over several of the classic tenets of traditional conservatism. Without being so bold as to make any dogmatic pronouncements on the true nature of man, we try to suggest that he is ultimately neither as rational as many behaviorists would have us believe nor as incapable of rational response to social problems as many who see only human depravity would like us to think. We close by affirming that the tension between man's nature and God's design which is built into our life in a society of men in a universe created by God is one of the most exciting as well as vexing phenomena with which men in politics have to deal. We hope that the final chapter points toward a new respect for both politics, where conflicting visions of the good are compromised if not reconciled, and morality, which infuses politics with purpose and reminds us that God does indeed have a design, however obscure it may seem at times to mortal men.

LEGISLATION AND THE WILL OF GOD

by *Congressman*
JIM WRIGHT

JIM WRIGHT

Congressman Jim Wright, now in his eighth term as Democratic Representative from Fort Worth, Texas, is regarded by his colleagues as one of the most effective debaters and able legislators in the House of Representatives. A man of broad interests, he has sponsored major national legislation dealing with water-pollution abatement, Latin American relations and economic development. The late President Kennedy once said of his record in the House, "I know of no city in the United States that is better represented in the Congress than Fort Worth."

Congressman Wright has been an active churchman. A Presbyterian elder, he is a former member of the Permanent Judicial Commission of his denomination's General Assembly. For several years he taught the Couples' Class at Washington's New York Avenue Presbyterian Church, and he is a frequent contributor to religious periodicals. He is the author of two books, *You and Your Congressman* and *The Coming Water Famine,* and articles in such journals as *Harper's, The Saturday Evening Post, This Week,* and *Coronet.*

Legislation and the Will of God

In September, 1964, the House was debating the first appropriation of money for the antipoverty program. Advocates recited the stark statistics of grisly want in the midst of affluence. Democratic spokesmen rhapsodized upon our unrivaled opportunity to "heal the gaping sores of economic denial" and "banish poverty from our land!" Some of us were thinking, What a chance to carry out that Scriptural mandate to feed the hungry and clothe the naked! To visit widows and fatherless in their affliction! Could anyone doubt we were doing the right thing?

Then Joel Broyhill, Republican Congressman from Virginia's Tenth District, entered the debate. Joel is a decent guy—friendly, energetic, hard-working, popular with both constituents and colleagues. But his speech ripped into some of my most cherished assumptions. Broyhill denounced the antipoverty program as the "most flagrant, unabashed vote-buying scheme I have seen in all my years in Congress." He scorned the very idea that the Federal government is capable of eliminating poverty. He quoted Scripture:

The Bible says, "For ye have the poor always with you" and while I do not wish to make an odious or offensive comparison,

I have a good deal more faith in the Bible than I have in some
politicians' promises!

Others in the House elaborated the Broyhill theme. Some
expressed deep concern over the increasingly popular fallacy
that "the world owes me a living." One voiced the view that
anyone who really wants to work can find a job, and another
hinted darkly that too easy access to goods without work
was "destroying the moral fibre" of the American people.
Someone charged that multiple welfare payments were encouraging illegitimate births—and darn near proved it. A
southern Democrat, leaning on the back railing of the House
chamber, peered over his glasses and grunted to a colleague:
"The Bible says if you don't work you don't eat!"

A couple of days later, the Washington *Post* editorially
excoriated Broyhill. In scathing sarcasm, the *Post* editorial
described the Virginia Congressman as that "noted theological and Biblical commentator," recounted his use of the
Scripture and concluded:

Mr. Broyhill has piously reconciled himself to his fat and
fortunate lot, and he expects the children of the poor to reconcile themselves with equal piety to their thin and miserable
one.

We await with great interest Mr. Broyhill's next sermon
which, according to a current rumor, will take as its text Matthew 19:24. As we remember it, no doubt imprecisely, the verse
warns, "It is easier for a camel to go through the eye of a
needle, than for a smug and complacent real estate operator with
political connections to enter the kingdom of God." If only the
same rule of admission were enforced in the halls of Congress.*

The tarbrush portrait, if unkind, was recognizable. Joel's
family is prominent in real estate. And financially successful.
Fat? Well, things are relative, you know. Pots and kettles

* *Washington Post,* Sept. 24, 1964, p. A-20.

and all that. Let's just say Joel outweighs me by ten pounds or so. (No need to mention he's at least a half inch taller . . .)

But if I'm tempted to pass moral judgment on either Joel Broyhill or the *Post* editorial writer for a lack of Christian charity in this case, they both might well retort: "Who the heck is Jim Wright to be so confounded self-righteous? We haven't heard *him* making any speeches against the *oil depletion allowance!* Did you know he took a political contribution from some truckers? And whatever else we need, we don't need some balding, bushy-eyebrowed Texas Democrat to lecture *us* on our moral responsibilities!"

And, much as I hate to say it, they'd have a point there. (It would be nicer, though, if they referred to me as "red-haired" instead of "balding." And as for my bushy—I mean my dramatic, forceful eyebrows—well, that just shows how prone some people are to abandon the issues and deal in cheap personalities.)

Several things need to be clear before we really try to get into the question of how a lawmaker can ascertain the divine will. Maybe the little story I've just recited illustrates a few of them. The first is that men of goodwill and sincere purpose often disagree. And this can happen without either antagonist being a sycophant, a demagogue or a rascal. Or even stupid, for that matter. None of us is given an exclusive franchise on God's truth, and we indulge a powerful presumption when we try to create God in our own images.

The second thing we need to recognize is that Congressmen are, after all, just people. The Congress is *of* the people. It is in one sense their mirror, and it reflects the aggregate strengths and weaknesses of the electorate. Its membership might include just about the same percentage of saints and sinners, fools and geniuses, rogues and heroes as does the general populace. The typical Congressman is a fairly average American—a bit better educated, a little more gregarious and considerably harder working than the norm, but still rather generally "representative." And this, after all, is his title as well as his description.

In sum, Congress is a collection of ordinary Americans grappling with extraordinary problems.

It is the problems that make our function unique—the almost infinite range and variety of them, the enormity of their consequences, and their sometimes baffling complexity. It is absolutely impossible for anyone to be a sufficient current authority on even most, let alone all, of the everchanging issues with which Congress must deal—the intricacies of the monetary system, the explosive uncertainties of the ghettos, the dilemmas of American agriculture, the volatile currents in the Middle East, the shifting patterns of power in Europe, the newest mood in the Kremlin, the brooding undertones of Southeast Asia, to name but a few. As soon as we think we've come to grips with one of these basic situations, the facts change in a cataclysmic and unexpected way, revealing the inadequacy of our knowledge and deflating our finest theories.

Yet we ordinary Americans must bring our very finite knowledge and fallible judgments to bear upon these problems. That is our job. The problems will not yield to simple, one-sentence solutions. Where are the clear moral absolutes, and how do they apply? Often there is truth on both sides. We can't just ponder and pontificate; we must vote! Two thousand bills will come before us in an average session. All have some importance. Perhaps one hundred are of major national consequence. Debate concluded, the clerk will call the roll. Often we'd like more time, more information. Sometimes we wish that we might answer, "Yes, but . . ." or

"No, if . . ." But as the roll is called, each Congressman's individual response must come as one unequivocal monosyllable. It is either "Yea" or "Nay," and that's that. Afterward, we hope that we were right.

What I'm saying is that if any group of people ever stood in *need* of the superhuman insights of divine revelation, it is we.

The third thing to know is that most Congressmen earnestly *want* to do the right thing. Few are theologians and fewer still are mystics, but most do have religious conviction. Cartoonists and jokesmiths to the contrary, a very appreciable number of legislators were inspired by idealism when they first decided to seek the office. It is a naïve politician perhaps who thinks he can change the course of the world dramatically, but most members were convinced that they could add something of value to the total political achievement of the nation. In my own case, I decided as a sophomore in high school that I wanted someday to serve in the Congress and to help create the foundations of a peaceful world.

Perhaps my case is revealing if not altogether typical. In my youth I was very certain in my vision of the road to world peace and of what I conceived to be my "mission in life." Like Moses, I would lead people from the bondage of war and oppression into Isaiah's promised day when men would "beat their swords into plough-shares, and their spears into pruning-hooks" (Isaiah 2:4, KJV). I'd be an architect of Tennyson's Parliament of Man where war drums throbbed no longer and battle flags were furled. I'd fulfill Woodrow Wilson's Fourteen Points and Franklin Roosevelt's Four Freedoms. It was all extremely heady stuff. I was young.

I was, frankly, intolerant of conflicting views. Though I wouldn't have admitted it and was probably clever enough that it didn't surface too visibly, I had a sort of messiah complex which, if forgivable in youth, can be insufferably dangerous in a public official. I hadn't yet learned that other people too were smart, and could be equally sincere while seeing things another way. I hadn't learned to walk the tightrope between self-righteousness and cynicism. Maybe I still haven't, but really that's the trick.

The next thing we ought to understand—and it has a bearing on what I've been saying—is the realistic limitation on what an individual lawmaker really can expect of himself. There was a time when I felt at one with Saint Paul's assertion, "I can do *all* things through Christ which strengtheneth me!" (Philippians 4:13, KJV). You know, I still accept that as a sort of philosophical abstraction; I wish I still could feel it as an absolute personal truth. (Maybe my trouble is just that I've had my 45th birthday.)

Actually, about the best that a good Congressman can reasonably hope for is to leave a decent footprint on the sands of progress. If he has done a good job, he will know, when he leaves Washington, that he has helped thousands of his constituents with their individual problems. He will have the satisfaction of realizing that he has accomplished some worthwhile things for his district. Perhaps he will rejoice in the fact that some of his ideas have become a permanent part of a major piece of legislation, even though someone senior to him (or perhaps of the opposite party) has been given the credit.

When the average Congressman completes his tenure of service, he will not really have changed the world much, but he will have seen important changes and will have participated to one extent or another in many of them. Remembering the thousands of individual services he has performed for people, the world leaders he has met, a few really good speeches he may have made on important issues, the hundreds of votes he has cast, the slice of history he personally has witnessed, he certainly will have the feeling that he made some contributions to the democratic process and to the shaping of his time.

No doubt it's just as well that this is so. The gradual dawning of legislative reality and the faint flawing of grandiose dreams can be effective antidotes to the terrible disease of *subucula inflata,* otherwise known as the stuffed shirt. It is, in fact, a terrible affliction, and politicians are peculiarly susceptible. Let me try to explain how.

A political career in a way is like the medieval ordeals which once were supposed to test the inner worth of an individual. Elective officialdom subjects its practitioner to a long series of subtle trials which have the capacity to bend and change his very character and to reveal its imperfections.

Many people, as I've said, enter the legislative arena impelled by some basic conviction of service to fellowman. Whether the individual's vision of a better world be true or false, clear and right or foggy and mistaken, is not the point right here. The point is that he *has* such a vision, worthy in his own mind of the dedication of a major part of his life.

He wouldn't say this to you, but he sees himself as a potential servant of cosmic forces—at least as an instrument through which good may come to his fellow creatures, perhaps as a possible agent of deity. Our fledgling lawmaker dreams of reforms, laws of his authorship which bring strength, beneficence and a better life to his land. Did he not so dream, why would he seek such an office? It all would be fatuous and empty, devoid of meaning.

Subtly and slowly, however, his dream of bringing off that reform begins to grow faint about the edges, dulled by reality, like the early-morning stars which fade and seem farther as the gray light of dawn appears. Major legislation, the Congressman discovers, is written by committee chairmen. And one gets to be a committee chairman by staying in Congress longer than all the others. But, as the star fades, something else takes its place.

People are constantly coming to our lawmaker for help, for advice, for intercession with administrative agencies of government. They keep telling him what a fine man he is, what a gracious fellow, what a real friend. While awaiting the opportunity to exercise important legislative craftsmanship, he *does* get some things done for his *district,* some local projects approved, some new jobs created. This is something. It is, after all, service of a sort. Sooner or later, they'll throw an Appreciation Dinner for him. They'll lionize him. And he'll discover, perhaps to his amazement, that he isn't embarrassed at all. He sort of *likes* it.

In the bright sunlight of personal acclaim, it's hard to keep the little stars of humility and altruistic service in one's vision. Nevertheless, our legislator rationalizes, if he can just hold on until seniority makes him a committee chairman, *then* he'll be able to make the great dreams come true. Therefore, naturally, it's important that he be reelected. It becomes a bit incongruous, then, to do his alms in private, lest like the flowers in Gray's "Elegy" they waste their sweetness on the desert air.

I recall the first time a public official suggested to me what I might say in introducing him for a speech and my shock at his immodesty. Now, after fourteen years in Congress, I send out mimeographed copies of a biographical summary to program chairmen where I'm slated for a speech. Well, technically, my office staff sends them out. But do you think I haven't read the summary, or that they'd send one of which I disapproved? I blush a little bit to tell you this. But not much. Not enough.

Press releases extolling a Congressman's accomplishments become a way of life. Try keeping your humility as you edit a press release, written about yourself in the third person, careful to give yourself the credit due. First thing you know, you'll start insisting they refer to your eyebrows as "forceful" instead of "bushy." At that point you'll know you have *subucula inflata*. Or—much worse—you'll have it and not know it!

The truth is that public office is just awfully hard on humility. We try to recapture it. We strike poses. We try to convince ourselves that we still possess it. We debate with the still, small voice and sometimes shout it down. Finally convinced that we're humble, we grow very *proud* of our humility. But feigned humility is worse than none at all. For it isn't only others but ourselves that we deceive.

How does this fit what we're saying? A fellow who has reached this point—and it's easy to do—is terribly vulnerable to one of the twin snares I've mentioned earlier: cynicism and self-righteousness. Either he decides it's all just a gaudy, worldly game after all, or he begins to believe his own propaganda and to invest his private judgments and opinions with a sort of divine infallibility. One can be as bad as the other.

Little need perhaps to dwell upon the dangers of political cynicism. If you were guilty of it, you probably wouldn't be reading this book. But let me make this plea: don't become cynical about politics. It is, in one sense, the only game in town!

Ridiculed in public print, satirized by cartoonist and comedian, butt of the street-corner humorist and self-righteous moralist alike, politics nevertheless is as necessary to the functioning of our society as water is to the flow of a river. It does not have to be filthy and corrupted —and neither does the river—for man has the means, if he has the will, to keep them both clean.

Politics is the lifeblood of democracy—the fuel that propels the engine of a free society. To profess love for the democratic form of government but disdain for politics is to pretend to honor the product while despising the process that creates it. The extent to which the political life of our country becomes corrupted is the result almost entirely of the tendency of sincere and decent people to wash their hands of the responsibility, like Pontius Pilate, and abdicate the field to the cynical.

More than 175 years ago, Andrew Oliver said in Boston:

Politics is the most hazardous of all professions. There is not another in which a man can hope to do so much good to his fellow creatures; neither is there any in which by a mere loss of nerve he may do such widespread harm; nor is there another in which he may so easily lose his own soul; nor is there another in which a positive and strict veracity is so difficult. But danger is the inseparable companion of honor. With all the temptations and degradations that beset it, politics is still the noblest career any man can choose.

I believe that. If I didn't believe it, I'd be doing something else. And I *should* be. So much for the snare of cynicism.

What of the other danger, the danger of self-righteous presumption? History shows us. In almost every age, there have been zealots, fanatics and pompous egocentrics who claim they have seen the vision of holiness and have been called to enforce it in the political arena. Often they've been completely sincere. Saul of Tarsus before his conversion felt a sanctimonious urge to persecute Christians. He went about it with the zeal of a Joe McCarthy hunting

Communists. The Crusades, the Spanish Inquisition, the witch burners of early Massachusetts, John Brown—all claimed a religious justification. Perhaps all were convinced they were doing God's will.

The sad and checkered tale of ecclesiastical history in the last 2,000 years gives evidence that few tyrannies are worse than that of tyrannical churchmen acting out of a sense of divine, infallible mission. The Jews persecuted the Christians before the Christians suffered martyrdom at the hands of the Roman Empire. After the Empire was Christianized, the Jewish people endured some 1,200 years of persecution from devout Christians all over Europe. Catholic officialdom persecuted Protestants, who later persecuted Catholics. Episcopalians and Presbyterians killed one another in bloody battles. Most thought they were doing the will of God.

A friend of mine has a watch his father took from a German soldier in World War I. Its inscription: *"Gott mit uns"!* The Japanese kamikaze pilots in World War II believed they were ensuring their hereafter by crash-diving their planes into American ships. And, of course, we felt so strongly that God was on *our* side. Or as heavyweight champion Joe Louis put it: "We're on God's side."

But Lincoln recognized in his Second Inaugural that "Both read the same Bible and pray to the same God, and each invokes His aid against the other. It may seem strange . . . but let us judge not, that we be not judged." Many Northerners did judge, of course, and so did Southerners.

And if you think self-righteous fanaticism is confined to the hawks of this world, you just don't know the hawkish doves. In March of 1969 a group of self-anointed young men affecting the clerical garb of monks broke into and physically wrecked the offices of the Dow Chemical Company in Washington. They thought of themselves as avenging angels and considered their act of vandalism to be above the law. After all, they were for "Peace!" So no doubt with many who've shouted down speakers, physically intimidated college faculties, and set fire to buildings on university campuses. So just and righteous do they deem their cause that they consider themselves exempt from any responsibility to the restraints of charity, humility, and the forbearance so necessary to the functioning of a free society.

Perhaps these examples seem terribly extreme to have relevance in a dissertation on the moral judgments of Congress. They are necessary to indicate the enormous danger of presumptive moral judgments in the political arena. To become completely convinced of the infallibility of one's personal predilections on a secular political issue is to play God, to assume to oneself the attributes of deity. It cultivates an arrogant intolerance of dissenting viewpoints and thus relegates one's political adversaries to the category of evil per se. In a parliamentary democracy, this attitude can be deadly.

Ben Franklin put it well. Toward the end of the Constitutional Convention in 1787, he told his fellow delegates: "I have experienced many instances of being obliged by better information, or fuller consideration, to change opinions even on important subjects." He pleaded that each delegate "would with me, on this occasion, *doubt a little of his own infallibility. . . .*"

Compromise—not necessarily a dirty word—is the very essence of the legislative process. Henry Clay said, "Do not despise compromise. It is the cement that holds the Union together." Those who scorn the art of conciliation and consider it somehow lacking in principle simply do not understand the business of lawmaking. Absolutists tend to hold compromise in rich contempt. Some even think it cowardly. But I'd warn them that they scoff loftily if unknowingly at man's most cherished political compromise —the Constitution of the United States. To condemn compromise is to blaspheme the steadying hands of moderation with which those thirty-eight memorable Americans penned that deed to freedom.

That the framers of the Constitution conciliated and compromised until they found a consensus does not mean that they lacked conviction. To the crucible full of conviction that man ought to be free, they applied the pestle of their collective experience, their fear of too great a central power, their scorn of one too weak. They had lived fretfully through both, and they wanted neither.

One cannot read Madison's Notes on that Constitutional Convention nor Elliott's Debates, which record the trials of its ratification, without being acutely aware of compromise on every page, conciliation in every paragraph. Who among us now would charge that they violated principle? Instead, we have created shrines to the very principles they evolved: the Federal union of states, tripartite central government, and the Bill of Rights . . . a democracy within a republic. They built an instrument of government worthy to endure, and all of it was the product of compromise.

The thought recalls the drama of the fateful afternoon of March 7, 1850, in the Senate of the United States. Daniel Webster, turning aside from his own abolitionist supporters, rose in the chamber and spoke to the hushed audience . . . "not as a Massachusetts man," he said, "nor as a Northern man, but as an American and a member of the Senate of the United States . . . I speak today for the preservation of the Union." Webster then proceeded to give to the Clay Compromise the support of his magnificent talents—and to the nation ten more years of internal peace. What chance he had for his party's Presidential nomination fled with the last syllable of that speech.

Is a man less honorable or does he have less courage who, heeding the voices of both extremes, partakes of each and acts for the sake of all? On the contrary, it often requires far greater courage to stand against the howling winds of mob hysteria and refuse to be stampeded by the thundering hooves of an unreasoning conformity.

Few have endured so much contemporaneous abuse from friend and foe alike as Abraham Lincoln; yet few have left their character so clearly etched upon our history. Lincoln was despised alike by the proslavery Southerners and the fanatical abolitionists. He was repudiated by members of his own party. For compromise was the soul of his offering; conciliation was his policy; moderation was his plea. To unite and thus preserve America was his single goal.

It was not that Lincoln loved his party less; it was that he loved his country more. It was not that he lacked conviction, but rather that he had conviction of a higher sort. His heart was too big for hatred, his view too broad for petty argumentation, his philosophy too deep to be confined by any of the glib labels of his day. His one consuming passion was to save the Union.

This is our common heritage. It is the business of democratic government to promote orderly progress, to synthesize a position which will satisfy the wishes of the responsible majority while protecting the rights of the most implacable minority. This must be the responsibility of political leadership. Unless we are constructive, we are of no use. Unless we cultivate a disposition to submerge petty differences and find areas of responsible agreement on which the reasonable and sensible majority can unite, we are impotent. As we fail in this, we fail America.

In the legislator's job, then, it is far more important

than in most vocations that we be on guard against self-righteous presumption. The more one becomes an absolutist, the more intractable one is in the positive rightness of his own position, the less likely he is to make any positive contribution to fashioning the workable compromise which is the warp and woof of legislation. Each of us in this business must, it seems to me, reserve in his mind the possibility that there may be some truth on the other side. And if the legislative process is to work, each of us must be ready to acknowledge that sincerity *does* exist on the other side.

How do we reconcile this necessity with the idea of profound moral conviction? Certainly not by abandoning our convictions. Each of us must work as hard as he can and argue as persuasively as he can for the positions he believes to be right. But he must not play God. He must not arrogate to himself the presumption of almighty wisdom. He must be very slow to pass harsh moral judgment upon those whose convictions disagree with his. He must proceed from an assumption that his antagonist is as sincere as he and may indeed have a thought worth considering.

There are people in the Congress with whom I almost always disagree on major legislation. Take James B. Utt of California or H. R. Gross of Iowa. They are Republicans; I am a Democrat. In the glib and superficial labeling which has become current in newspaper practice, they are "conservative," while I guess I am a "progressive" or a "moderate" or something like that. Both Jimmy Utt and H. R. Gross are churchmen. I am not in any position to question the genuineness of their convictions or the sincerity of their moral concern with social issues.

But we do very profoundly disagree. Utt thinks we ought to "get the U.S. out of the U.N. and the U.N. out of the U.S." I regard the U.N. with all its imperfections as mankind's best existing hope for peace. I get emotionally involved with the future of Latin America and am determined to consider its possibilities hopeful. H. R. Gross believes it's largely a lost cause. Gross actively opposes most social legislation—Federal aid to schools, medical care for the elderly, aid to the strife-torn cities, etc. I support this legislation. Certain of my colleagues from the deep South vote for some of these social-welfare programs, but vote against civil-rights bills while I am voting for them. How do we reconcile our widely varying conceptions of the Christian's social duty?

The idea of revelation is deeply imbedded in Christianity. If the Creator is omnipotent, as we say he is, then the source of infallible judgments must be right here somewhere for us to tap. There has to be a socket into which we can screw our bulbs and show forth the light of perfect truth. Yet, for most of us imperfect creatures it isn't quite that simple.

Is it possible that the Creator in his infinite wisdom makes Utts and Wrights, Goldwaters and Humphreys, internationalists and isolationists, liberals, conservatives and moderates in the precise electoral proportion to accomplish his will? Could it be that he shows to each of us a part of the truth, and then "stacks the deck" so to speak, so as to achieve the result he foreordains in some mysterious and inexplicable way on a scale of probabilities and a timetable beyond our mortal comprehension? Is it conceivable that the whole thing resembles a gambling parlor at Las Vegas where—whatever happens on an individual spin—the house is bound to win out in the end? That's a possibility at least. The conclusion may be tempting to some of us Presbyterians—predestination and all that. But somehow I can't quite think it works just that way either.

For one thing, I just don't believe that God intended for

people to hate and kill each other. I don't think he ordained for some to live in misery and pain and want or for any to die of starvation. I can't conceive that he purposes for some to be hounded and persecuted by others. These things just do not square with my conception of a loving Creator. I believe he intends his creatures to work for peace among men, for a just and compassionate social order, for reconciliation of differences between people of different races, different nations, different religions, different social strata, even between men of different generations. "Blessed are the peacemakers" may apply with particular force to members of Congress.

I take quite literally Saint Paul's description of the Almighty as one who created "of one blood all the nations of men for to dwell on all the face of the earth" (Acts 17:26, KJV). I think he intends for us mortal creatures to patch up our differences, to love one another, to banish selfishness and evil, and to see that none of his creatures is mistreated. That is a tall order and we haven't achieved it, but I think the eternal wisdom purposes that we do so. And I believe these goals are to be attained not only through individual deeds of individual humans but in society as well and in the social structures that we create.

None of this has come to me in a blinding flash of light as to Saint Paul on the road to Damascus or as to Moses in a voice from a burning bush. It just happens to be the way I conceive of the universe and the purposes of God. It is the only logical set of assumptions I can equate with the great commandment to love the Lord thy God and love thy neighbor as thyself.

But how do we go about achieving this perfect state of things with laws which must of necessity bear the frailties and imperfections of their authors? I have some personal ideas about that from time to time, but so do my equally conscientious colleagues. Sometimes our ideas differ. When I start delineating all the specifics of how to achieve these divine ends, I begin to get in trouble.

Even churches get in trouble. They don't always agree with one another. Individual denominations sometimes disagree internally. When a group of denominations bands together and seeks consensus, it—like as not—will encounter opposition from an adversary grouping. The National Council of Churches has offered guidelines on a broad variety of legislative fronts. Now comes a consortium of more Fundamentalist denominations, calling itself the American Council of Christian Churches, and blasts the NCC as "one of the most dangerous groups in America," accusing it of promoting what the ACC views as the triplet sins of modernism, socialism and ecumenism.

Do you see what troubles we poor mortal Congressmen confront? At my age maybe I can go along, up to a point, with those who are irritated by modernism, and as a somewhat general matter I am opposed to socialism, but when they start jumping on ecumenism, then I think they have quit preaching and gone to meddling. (Me, I'm an ecumenicist—a *Presbyterian* ecumenicist, of course.)

★ ★ ★

In all seriousness and in total candor, it is no easy matter for a legislative body to be certain of its place in interpreting moral issues. The problem has haunted and hounded mankind almost since the beginning of the race. We have frequently fumbled in our efforts to locate the precise point at which the rights of society begin and those of the individual leave off. This question has challenged the most learned legal and theological minds of all ages.

Laws by their nature contain restraints. That is a primary purpose of law. The truly ideal society would be one in which no legally enacted moral restraint would be necessary. Everybody would do the right thing *voluntarily*. Yet it needs no argument that this sanguine state of affairs has not yet arrived.

So it is the business of law to impose restraints. But what restraints? Nobody will question that society needs to protect its members from injury by such obvious crimes as theft, murder, assault, or kidnapping, for example. A state with no such restrictions based upon commonly accepted moral fundamentals of right and wrong would be anarchy in its rankest form.

By the same token, we surely would find general public agreement today that no one group in our society has any right to force its own particular predilections of morality upon society as a whole, no matter how deeply held its convictions may be. A Federal law prohibiting contraception, for example, would provoke open opposition as an attempt to impose the convictions of one ecclesiastical order upon the rest of society. Similarly, most people recognize today that a law would contravene our most basic legal concepts if it sought to prohibit dancing or card playing or movies on Sunday afternoon, although in an earlier time many communities invoked such ordinances because religious people found these practices objectionable.

If a man would protect himself and his family against forceful observance of the moral beliefs of others, must he not then protect others against being legally forced to observe his own? So what is the proper function of society in upholding and defending public morality by legal enactment? The great difficulty always lies in making differentiations between that which is truly harmful and dangerous to society and that which is merely distasteful to ourselves. And the great danger lies in the fact that laws must be written and administered by fallible human beings.

The preponderant majority of public sentiment, for example, will surely agree on the need for some laws to protect the public sensitivity and particularly the unsuspecting young from offensive obscenity. My mail is heavy —and so is that of most Congressmen—with disgusting enclosures which invaded the mailboxes of constituents, sent now to me with expressions of outrage. Yet those who have attempted to write laws defining what is and is not obscene know the difficulty which this task poses. In the end the courts must make a separate determination in each case.

Enforcement of such laws becomes a problem in itself. During my tenure in the Congress, we have four times enacted statutes to impose penalties upon the distribution of lewd and salacious literature and pictorials through the U.S. mails. The most revolting advertisement of such wares had sometimes been sent unsolicited to entire mailing lists of young people. No sooner had the anguished cries of outraged parents reached the enforcement authorities and mailing privileges of the offending firms been revoked, than the smut merchants had moved to other towns and set up their operations under different names. That the offending publishers would incur such repeated inconveniences and risk heavy fines to pursue so depraved an activity indicates one disturbing fact: financially it was paying off. What can any legislative body do to reform the tastes and morals of the entire citizenry and thus make such nefarious activities unremunerative? The answer, of course, is relatively little.

This has been true since the beginning. Unless people are led to *want* to obey laws, they find ways to evade them. This is true even in a repressive police state with its reprehensible crimes against human dignity. So much more is it true in a free society which rests its case upon a faith in its public and in the assumption that most people will willingly respect and obey laws which are not unduly repressive of their rights.

Some of the earliest attempts at legislating morality stemmed apparently from the belief that it was somehow sinful to indulge oneself in luxuries. Nor can this notion be laid exclusively to Puritanism, or even to Christian ethics. Long before the Christian age, Greeks of the Spartan influence sought to limit legally the type and amount of furniture a man might keep in his house. In the year 215 B.C., the Romans passed a law prohibiting women from possessing more than one-half ounce of gold or from wearing dresses of more than one color. And in 161 B.C. the serving of fowl was prohibited, "except for one hen unfattened." This body of law, equating austerity with righteousness, came to be known as sumptuary law. If the purpose of these laws was basically economic, at least they were advocated and defended on grounds of morality.

Such taste statutes persisted well into the Christian age, took renewed fervor and became extensive throughout Europe during the Middle Ages and after. Nürnberg legally regulated extravagant dress, with stringent restrictions against peaks on shoes, which apparently were thought to be provocative of low and base thoughts. One regulation then in vogue might appeal to parents of modern teenagers. It prohibited "any but the customary dances which have come down of old."

An unexpected reverse twist is seen in certain European statutes of the time which sought to regulate—of all things —men's clothing. The particular object of public opprobrium was the shortening of the jacket above the knees. Apparently this offended the taste of some folks then in the same manner as the modern miniskirt or the plunging neckline in women's apparel.

In 1520, three men were actually executed in Switzerland for swearing. The government encouraged people to inform on violators. Sunday laws prohibited card playing but permitted rifle and crossbow practicing. In Zurich, silk borders on bodices were outlawed and legally confiscated, but oddly two classes were specifically exempted—women of aristocratic guilds and "public prostitutes." England outlawed the wearing of furs by women. It hardly needs to be observed that these laws occurred before the day of women's suffrage!

As might be expected, these taste statutes which sought to bring about marked changes in public habits by legislation almost always failed. It is easy enough for us in retrospect to scoff at the now rather apparent futility of such efforts. With the benefit of several hundred years of hindsight and almost two hundred years of experience in religious freedom, we see several obvious flaws.

First of all, we see in them an almost shocking lack of faith in the public and in such civilizing nongovernmental influences as the church and the family to provide leadership in such voluntary matters of public taste and morals. Secondly, we might stand astonished at the arrogance and presumption of medieval lawmakers who invoke the name of God in attempting to force their own private tastes upon others. It seems a rather clear case of men attempting to make God in their own image!

Yet it would be well for us to remember that religious freedom as we know it did not spring full blown even in America until after this country had undergone nearly one hundred years of sad and mottled experience with official state churches and the inevitable repressions of freedom which this almost always meant.

It seems ironic that this country, composed largely of people who had fled the tyranny of religious persecutions and wars that had terrorized Europe for nearly two hundred years, did not automatically establish total religious freedom. Yet, humanly enough, once they had settled, most of our forebears fell into the very patterns from which they had fled. Every colony except Pennsylvania and Rhode Island had an officially established state church, and almost without exception the laws of the colonies discriminated against dissenters from that church. Persecution, witch hunts, heresy hunts began to break out with appalling frequency. Thoughtful men wondered if the blood baths of Europe were going to flame anew on this continent. Fortunately, there was a Thomas Jefferson and enough men of vision and goodwill to follow the leadership he represented.

And so for almost two centuries we as a nation have sought to keep such legal enactments to a necessary minimum.

Ruskin said the strength of a society may be measured by the amount of *persuasion* which can be used as opposed to the amount of *force* that is necessary. The test of a man or of a nation is what he or it will do when not forced to do anything. The English moralist Hobbes put it this way: "To force morality by threat of punishment is to confront the individual with a choice between *two evils,* not a choice between good and evil."

All Americans, and particularly those of us who hold strong convictions, need to be on guard constantly against the ugly temptation to assign impure motives to others who simply disagree with us, thus enthroning our personal opinions and mistaking our own prejudices for holiness. The ultimate blasphemy is to attempt to make oneself God. Judge Learned Hand once said that the spirit of liberty is the spirit which is not too sure that it is right.

Certain general guidelines may be helpful. First of all,

the law exists not for the propagation of one set of ideas against another, but rather for the protection of society. Second, the basic purpose of law is not to punish criminals but to prevent crime. It is successful law only insofar as it accomplishes this purpose. Third, the law per se is concerned not with internal attitudes but with external conduct. Motives are not normally the concern of the law; they belong to the individual conscience. Finally, law in the Western tradition is essentially limited. Constitutions exist for the purpose of limiting rather than expanding the application of law.

What, then, are some of the particular areas of proper legal responsibility? We have already mentioned the need to protect the public against the flaunting of unwanted obscenity. Similarly, the nation has determined that all traffic in narcotics must in the public interest be subject to extremely stringent controls. On almost all counts of the definition stated above, forced restraint against traffic in narcotics surely qualifies as a proper area of public enforcement.

In an age of mass merchandising when the public lies largely at the mercy of information and claims disseminated by advertisers, and when those same advertisers to a large extent control the very media of public communication, society has found laws necessary to protect the public against fraudulently misleading and fundamentally untruthful advertising.

Often the mere threat of public censure will serve to make certain industries clean up their own backyards rather than submit to public control. One example is the television industry. All of us were appalled a few years ago to learn that we had been taken in by rigged contests. While there was nothing unlawful about this, surely nobody could contend that it was anything less than fundamentally dishonest. Hearings were conducted by Congressional committees. As a result the television industry voluntarily imposed its own prohibitions against such deception.

I happen to be one of those who feels that television as a whole still exhibits far too much violence to be an altogether healthy influence. Yet, I am free to influence what programs my minor children view over television. Not only am I free to do so, as a parent I think I have a responsibility to do so.

Television has an unrivaled capacity to become either a great elevater or a great leveler. To overestimate its potential for good or bad would be difficult indeed. But in a free society the control that can properly be exercised by law is limited. Although television and radio, as a collection of licensees using the public airwaves, are properly subject to certain restrictions which do not apply to movies, magazines and newspapers, any attempt by government to regulate program content would smack of thought control. If the American people made it clear that they did not *want* so much exposure to sex and violence, however, it no longer would be profitable for any of the media to exhibit so much.

The same may be said of books. I am appalled at the apparent belief on the part of writers and publishers that the surest way to have a best seller is to fill a book with pointless filth. Yet, apparently, there is some basis for that conclusion. As repelled as many of us personally may be by the themes of depravity and perversion contained in some best sellers, I must say in candor that apparently the most successful way to sell a book is to get it talked about by reviewers, banned in Boston, or challenged in the courts.

As distasteful as this fact is to me, I fear even more

deeply the other extreme in which we would set up public censors under the aegis of government to tell the public what it may or may not read. This could lead to the most detestable forms of thought control, moving insidiously and perhaps inevitably from attempted moral censorship into the field of political censorship. If any churchman should be tempted to desire general public censorship of books and periodicals beyond that encompassing only the flagrantly and incontestably obscene, then he ought to re-call the fact that history's first and most vigorous attempts to prohibit publishing of the printed word were directed against the publishing of the Holy Scriptures themselves.

What it all comes to is that government by compulsion can only prevent certain overt abuses. Government can and must protect society against clear and unmistakable danger. Yet the fundamental truth remains that morality is not changed by law.

A corollary truth, however, also remains: society *is* changed by morality. This is the fundamental distinction between political action and religious action. The politician may say, "There ought to be a law." But the Christian churchman will say, "There ought to be a change; there-fore, let it begin with me."

Hasn't there been a curious omission in this part of our discussion? We have talked almost wholly in terms of the "thou shalt not's." We have hardly mentioned the "thou shalt's." Yet morality and social ethics are concerned with both. The law by its very nature is a negative thing in the areas of prohibitions and sanctions and penalties.

Yet Christianity is not a negative thing. It is a positive thing. Its essence is not found in the stale and hidebound prohibitions of the Pharisees. It is not found among the whited sepulchers. It is found in the clean fresh air and under the open skies where humanity first breathed the incomparable fragrance of the Sermon on the Mount and felt the harsh and restrictive chains of legal obedience fall away in the new freedom of love for all mankind.

And so it is with a nation and its morality. Its security lies not in mistrust but in faith. Its strength is never founded on fear but on hope. Its power derives not from hate but from love, from charity. We Christians claim to be heirs to the hope of the world. To our safekeeping has been entrusted the mustard seed, the leaven for the loaf. Are we concerned about public morality? Perhaps we might do well to think more in terms of what constructive things we ourselves must do and less in terms of what we would force others not to do. The heart of our faith is that God deals with man in the realm of the unenforceables, that he transforms society through individuals, not individuals through society.

Members of Congress are individuals. It is our job in life to speak and act for a lot of other individuals. But we need ever to be conscious of our limitations. We cannot *create* the ideal society. Perhaps the best we can create is a legal *climate* conducive to its development. We can outlaw obvious evils. We can try to see that no citizen of this land is deprived of his just rights. We can strive by political means to guarantee that every child, created in God's image, shall have a fair and full chance to develop his own potential for good—and the broadest opportunity to express it. By deed and word, as it is given to us to see the truth, we can work for peace among men. And we can hope that our wisdom is not folly.

As has been said by Paul Tillich, we live in two orders. All history tells us that the political order will not really change the spiritual order. But the spiritual order, when its conviction is deep enough and its dedication true enough, will ultimately and immutably and supremely change the political order. This is our hope.

Meanwhile, what do we fellows in Congress do about all this? Well, we just do the best we can. A Member of Congress, fallible and mortal, can contribute to the fulfillment of this hope. He can if he will balance the awareness of his power with an awareness of his human limitations. He can if, with Saint Francis, he seeks first to understand rather than to be understood, to love rather than to be loved.

Empowered to determine what others must render unto Caesar, the lawmaker first might ask what he himself may render unto God. For the face of the coin bears Caesar's image, but that of man bears the image of his Creator. The coin performs its intended use only as it serves the will of the power that minted it. And so it is with man.

THE POLITICS
OF HUNGER

by Senator
GEORGE McGOVERN

GEORGE McGOVERN

A professor turned politician, Senator George McGovern of South Dakota has become widely known as a spokesman for the poor and disadvantaged. As chairman of the Senate Select Committee on Nutrition and Human Needs, he is the Senate's leading expert on the problem of hunger. He entered politics in 1956, when he won election to the House of Representatives. In 1961 he was named director of Food for Peace and special assistant to President John F. Kennedy, and the following year he was elected to the Senate, where he sits on the Agriculture and Interior Committees and the Subcommittee on Indian Affairs. He is chairman of the Democratic National Reform Commission, and in 1968 was a candidate for the Democratic Presidential nomination.

The son of a Methodist minister, Senator McGovern has long been active as a lay leader in the church. He is the author of three books: *War Against Want* (1964), *Agricultural Thought in the Twentieth Century* (1967), and *A Time of War/A Time of Peace* (1968), and has been a regular contributor to such leading magazines as *Look,* the *Atlantic Monthly, The Saturday Review, The New Republic, The New York Times* magazine, and *Commentary.*

The Politics of Hunger

"I don't know, Orville," said Robert Kennedy to Secretary of Agriculture Freeman; "I'd just get the food down there. I can't believe that in this country we can't get some food down there." With this expression of disbelief, a United States Senator summed up the growing frustration of those who believe it is morally indefensible to permit millions of people to go hungry in a country which produces six hundred tons of food per minute.

There seems little point, in the year 1970, in rehashing the moral argument against allowing hunger to continue. Far more important than a lengthy moral debate against the few who still feel that any assistance demeans its recipients, or who object to delivery of assistance by government, is an understanding of why a broad moral consensus favoring an end to hunger in America has failed to produce that end. For the simple fact is that several years after severe malnutrition and hunger were rediscovered in America, the niceties of consensus politics threaten to turn the battle against hunger into little more than a protracted series of ineffectual skirmishes.

I believe that to understand this failure is to understand both a major strength and a critical weakness of the American political system. It is to understand that in America we have devised a governmental system which is almost totally unable to deal with problems in moral terms. When fed into the American political process, an essentially ethical or moral issue is quickly shorn of its moral component. It becomes, instead, a practical problem which is studied, debated, and slowly, very slowly, dealt with in whatever way seems least likely to disturb the existing order. As often as not, it is simply talked to death.

This process of improvisation and delay has worked with surprising regularity in the past. It has generally bought time, and time has brought a weakening of moral passion and a moderate consensus on how best to proceed.

But delay and compromise have not always worked. Though they have often won agreement, there have been times when they have led only to anger and deepening crisis. In the decade preceding the Civil War, and again in the decade of the 1960's, the failure of government to abandon gradual compromise for moral leadership aggravated, rather than moderated, the great issue of the day.

Hunger in America is a part of the great domestic issue of this decade. That issue, overlaid and sharpened by the race problem, is whether or not the world's first affluent *majority* will respond to the problems of history's first poor *minority*. For the first time the power of the poor, no matter how angry they become, is not in itself sufficient to bring them political victory. Instead they must count on help from outside their ranks. A key factor in getting this help must be an ethically motivated conviction that such help should be provided. Such a belief must not only exist, it must be strong enough to prod the believer into political action, and this action must produce an effective response from government.

There is no question in my mind that most Americans do believe this assistance should be provided. From the teaching "Each man his brother's keeper," most of us would infer a responsibility to make food available to the hungry wherever possible, and especially in this land of over-abundance. Whenever this need has seemed clear, as most recently in Biafra, Americans have seen an equally clear obligation to feed the hungry.

As a layman who has tried to find practical applications for my faith, I believe that the Christian bears a special responsibility on issues such as this one. When a moral imperative such as the elimination of hunger is blunted by laxity, indifference or conscious delay, he must bring to bear the demands of his Christian conscience, in an attempt to refocus our moral sensitivities to the most urgent problems of our own day. The Biblical mandate could not be clearer on this point. Jesus himself, foretelling the Day of Judgment to the disciples in the Gospel according to St. Matthew, said:

Then shall [the King] say also unto them on the left hand, Depart from me, ye cursed, into everlasting fire, prepared for the devil and his angels:

For I was an hungered, and ye gave me no meat: I was thirsty, and ye gave me no drink:

I was a stranger, and ye took me not in: naked, and ye clothed me not: sick, and in prison, and ye visited me not.

Then shall they also answer him, saying, Lord, when saw we thee an hungered, or athirst, or a stranger, or naked, or sick, or in prison, and did not minister unto thee?

Then shall he answer them, saying, Verily, I say unto you, Inasmuch as ye did it not to one of the least of these, ye did it not to me.

Matthew 25:41–45, KJV

Or again in the Old Testament, as God spoke to the Children of Israel through the prophet Isaiah:

Is not *this* the fast that I have chosen? to loose the bands of wickedness, to undo the heavy burdens, and to let the oppressed go free, and that ye break every yoke?

Is it not to deal thy bread to the hungry, and that thou bring the poor that are cast out to thy house? when thou seest the naked, that thou cover him; and that thou hide not thyself from thine own flesh?

Then shall thy light break forth as the morning, and thine health shall spring forth speedily: and thy righteousness shall go before thee; the glory of the Lord shall be thy rereward.

Isaiah 58:6–8, KJV

Traditionally Christians have interpreted passages such as these as an invitation to private charitable giving. And indeed such activity is entirely appropriate and as much needed today as it has always been. But the plain fact is that, while many earnest Christians have taken this Biblical mandate to heart and practiced private benevolence to the point of real personal sacrifice, still the overall impact of private charity, through the church and other organizations, has not made a significant dent in the problem of widespread hunger and malnutrition which is found in many regions of our nation. Given the urgency and size of the task, I believe that only government, of all our private and public agencies, has enough resources and operates on a large enough scale to attack this problem at its roots.

What then is the conclusion for the Christian? Plainly, the answer is not that every Christian should leap into politics or government to do battle against the forces of sloth, indifference and avarice. But I would submit that the Christian has an obligation to think soberly and to exercise careful and prayerful judgment on public issues, candidates and programs. This means not simply voting, but bringing faith to bear in a practical way by attempting to influence the quality and direction of our political programs.

Nowhere is this need more evident than in the case of hunger. As the most painful and obvious symptom of poverty, hunger is the issue on which the poor should enjoy the greatest success. Their own organized efforts to fight hunger should, theoretically, touch off the same national moral outrage that greeted hunger in Biafra. This national outrage, combined with our undoubted ability to end hunger immediately, should—again theoretically—produce action. But a careful look at how the hunger issue has actually developed reveals a partial flaw in this theory. It shows that our political system does not respond effectively to a moral imperative, even when that imperative is accepted by a solid majority of our people.

Before turning to recent efforts to deal with the hunger problem, it is important to note that these efforts do not constitute the first organized attack on malnutrition in America. Testifying before the Senate Select Committee on Nutrition and Human Needs, Dr. Margaret Mead told of a comprehensive wartime nutrition program. By the end of World War II, she said,

> Nutrition had become a word that nobody dared to be against—like motherhood. We had set up entirely new patterns of eating in many parts of the country where we had the most deficient diets. We had wiped out the major deficiency diseases . . . and in the face of the affluence of the early 1950's, by 1960 it was possible to say that the major nutritional disease in the United States was overnutrition.

These successes were achieved, Dr. Mead added, at a time when knowledge of proper nutrition was far less extensive than it is today, and when our attention was focused on a life-or-death military struggle abroad. They were achieved, she continued, because government at all levels, private industry, the news media, voluntary agencies, and the people all agreed that malnutrition had to be stopped and cooperated toward that end.

What Dr. Mead failed to explain was why such broad agreement and cooperation existed during World War II. Why did the cooperating parties not argue then, as they do now, that Federal taxes were too high, local governments too poor, profit margins too low, or advertising space too costly to permit a major government-industry-media attack on hunger and inadequate nutrition? There are two answers to this question, and both of them shed light on the question why our recent responses to hunger have been so much less effective than the response our nation mounted in time of war.

The first answer is that during a major war, as at no other time, Americans suspend their normal gradualistic political approach to major national problems. In place of political debate they substitute an efficient problem-solving approach which ignores bureaucratic and political niceties in favor of rapid attainment of accepted goals. Ending hunger was such a goal, and the wartime system produced dramatic successes in meeting that goal.

The second reason for the success of the wartime anti-hunger campaign was that hunger then was not predominantly a moral issue. Rather, it was recognized that, as a practical matter, undernourished recruits and hungry factory hands were a hindrance to the war effort. With the fate of the nation hanging on the success of that effort, it was a relatively easy matter to mount and carry through a popular campaign against hunger.

In 1943 the United States government was geared for action, not debate, and it sought action against hunger as a wartime necessity, not a moral imperative. Today neither of these conditions exists. In their absence, the new debate over hunger in America looks much different from the old.

In December, 1968, Dr. Mead told the Select Committee on Nutrition and Human Needs:

> We need to face the simple facts: The American people are less well nourished, as a whole, than they were ten years ago.

During an eight-month period in 1969, Senators on the Select Committee heard testimony which established beyond doubt the existence of what I believe can only be called a national scandal. We learned that, at a time when our country spends billions of dollars to keep farmers from producing more food, hunger and malnutrition are causing permanent brain damage to many children, weakening their resistance to disease, stunting their growth, reducing their ability to learn or work, and sometimes even killing them. This hunger is not in Asia or Africa or Latin America; it is in Texas, New York, Louisiana, Kentucky, and every other state in our nation. It does not affect just a few; it afflicts up to fifteen million poor Americans and nearly 40 percent of all children from poor families. (The definition of "poor" used throughout this essay is the standard poverty index developed and used by the Office of Economic Opportunity: an annual income below $3,555 for a family of four.)

How can hunger on this scale possibly exist in the richest nation the world has ever known? How can a country that boasts the most effective food production and distribution system ever devised permit up to fifteen million of its citizens to suffer from malnutrition?

Until recently simple ignorance of the problem—although

a shocking indictment of the inability of our system to bring the needs of the poor to our notice—was an honest answer to this question. Following a massive effort to end malnutrition during the 1940's, Americans followed the classic pattern described by a witness before the Select Committee:

What we do in the United States is first to say that we face a terrible crisis. Then we roll up our sleeves and we do something about it, and we can do something about it very well and very fast. The worse it seems, the better we do. We then say we have done a wonderful job and relax and go somewhere else. . . . This is what we did with nutrition.

Since 1950 America has clearly been "somewhere else" with respect to proper nutrition for her citizens. Our reluctance to return to the problem of hunger has been due in part to a simple inability to believe, as we push our grocery carts down aisles lined with food of every description, that there are literally millions of Americans who have never seen the inside of a supermarket. Writing in the early 1960's, even Michael Harrington—hardly one to understate the failures of the Establishment—believed that hunger was one problem which had been solved in America.

But tramping the Mississippi Delta with the Senate Subcommittee on Employment, Manpower and Poverty, Senator Robert Kennedy could not agree. There in the Delta, the Senators saw starvation plain and simple. They learned that the choice facing many residents was one between outright starvation and moving north to the ghettos of Chicago, Detroit or New York. On their return they unanimously recommended to the President that an emergency be declared in Mississippi and that various steps be taken to meet this emergency.

This Senate Subcommittee trip established a public record of the existence of hunger, malnutrition, and even starvation in America. Since 1967 that record has grown continuously. Following up on the Senators' investigation, a team of six distinguished physicians toured the Delta in Mississippi. They included Dr. Joseph Brenner of the Massachusetts Institute of Technology; Dr. Robert Coles of Harvard University; Dr. Alan Mermann and Dr. Milton Senn, both of Yale University; Dr. Cyril Walwyn of Yazoo City, Mississippi; and Dr. Raymond Wheeler of Charlotte, North Carolina. In their report to the Senate, the doctors said:

> In Delta counties . . . we saw children whose nutritional and medical condition we can only describe as shocking—even to a group of physicians whose work involves daily confrontation with disease and suffering. In child after child we saw: evidence of vitamin and mineral deficiencies; serious untreated skin infestation and ulcerations; eye and ear diseases, also unattended bone diseases secondary to poor food intake; the prevalence of bacterial and parasitic disease, as well as severe anemia . . . in boys and girls in every county we visited, obvious evidence of severe malnutrition, with injury to the body's tissues—its muscles, bones, and skin as well as an associated psychological state of fatigue, listlessness, and exhaustion. . . .
>
> We saw children who don't get to drink milk, don't get to eat fruit, green vegetables, or meat. They live on starches—grits, bread, Kool Aid . . . in sum, we saw children who are hungry and who are sick—children for whom hunger is a daily fact of life and sickness, in many forms, an inevitability. We do not want to quibble over words, but "malnutrition" is not quite what we found. . . . They are suffering from hunger and disease and directly or indirectly they are dying from them— which is exactly what "starvation" means.

One year later, in April, 1968, the Citizens' Board of Inquiry into Hunger and Malnutrition in the United States published an independent study of malnutrition in this country. They estimated that fourteen million Americans were unable to obtain the food necessary to meet minimum nutritional standards. They utilized case histories, studies of particular areas, and national data in an appeal to Americans to recognize that the plight of these fourteen million demanded immediate consideration.

During that same month, April, 1968, the CBS television network aired its superb documentary entitled "Hunger in America." CBS repeated the charge that millions of Americans are seriously undernourished. A series of pathetic sequences showed the crippling effects of hunger on children in Alabama, on pregnant women in San Antonio, on tenant farmers in Virginia. Charles Kuralt closed the program with the simple hope that in this land of abundance "the most basic human need, food, might someday become a human right."

That this most basic human need was not yet a right in America was further dramatized by the Poor People's Campaign in the spring of 1968. By making an end to hunger the central theme of the campaign, Dr. Ralph Abernathy added the organized voice of the poor themselves to the growing public record of hunger in the United States.

Following the Poor People's Campaign, the Senate Select Committee on Nutrition and Human Needs resumed the writing of this record. At one of our first hearings Dr. Arnold Schaefer, director of the National Nutrition Survey of the United States Public Health Service, filled the one remaining gap in the argument that hunger is in fact a critical health hazard to millions of the poorest citizens of this country. When CBS had interviewed people who said they were hungry, the doubters had protested that such people were few in number and that CBS was trying to sensationalize a minor problem. But the sort of evidence that Dr.

Schaefer presented to the Select Committee could not be so easily dismissed. His National Nutrition Survey was a scientific study of thousands of families in ten states. It was conducted by trained medical personnel, whose findings were based not on scattered interviews but on thorough medical examinations, including blood samples, of a cross sampling of thousands of people living in these ten states.

Among Dr. Schaefer's preliminary findings, as reported to the Select Committee, were the following:

1. Some 34 percent of our poorer preschool children exhibit anemia which causes "fatigue, listlessness, an inability to perform" . . . and which is so serious that any doctor would pronounce its victims candidates for medical treatment.

2. Goiter, a disease which can be prevented for one quarter of a penny per person per year, exists in this country at a level classified by the World Health Organization as "endemic."

3. Growth retardation, often a companion to permanent brain damage, is common among children examined by the Public Health Service.

4. Vitamin A deficiency, unknown in any child who has enough milk to drink, afflicts 33 percent of the younger children of the poor.

5. Levels of malnutrition in poverty groups in the United States are "very similar" and "in some cases worse" than those in Latin America and other underdeveloped areas.

If ignorance of the problem has been one reason for our failure to end hunger in the past, it obviously should not be a factor today. A lengthy, carefully documented, widely publicized record is now available. Surveys taken in the spring of 1969 indicated that this record has, in fact, been read. In at least two samplings, over 75 percent of those interviewed said they believed that hunger is a significant problem for large numbers of poor citizens.

Coupled with this new awareness of the existence of

hunger is the growing realization that malnutrition poses a very serious hazard to health. Summarizing a public record nearly as long as that dealing with the incidence of malnutrition, the Select Committee on Nutrition and Human Needs recently reported that:

> . . . Hunger and malnutrition as found in this country, coupled with other social and economic factors, can and does have a direct and major adverse effect on the normal physical and mental development of its victims. . . . Malnutrition and undernutrition among poor American children can and does result in:
>
> —apathy, listlessness, and loss of energy and ability to concentrate, slowness of comprehension, inattention, restlessness, behavioral problems, and retarded learning among preschool and school children;
> —lowered resistance to disease and infection; and
> —general retardation in the mental and physical growth of children who are its victims.
>
> In short, the intellectual growth, learning capacity and physical capabilities of children among low-income families in the United States is seriously compromised by hunger and malnutrition.

With this finding the public record on hunger in America is complete. It has been proved, and widely accepted, that hunger and malnutrition affect millions of poor American families. It has also been shown that this hunger causes serious, often irreparable, damage—particularly to young children. What is now in doubt is not the fact, but the response that will be made to the fact, of hunger in America.

As public attention began to focus on the disturbing news that many people in America do not get enough food simply because they are too poor, the United States Department of Agriculture was the first government agency to come under criticism. For years it had been apparent that the Department's two major food assistance programs had serious shortcomings. But these programs, as Agriculture officials quickly noted, were never intended to provide adequate nutrition to millions of poor families. They were operated by the Agriculture Department rather than the Department of Health, Education and Welfare precisely because they were directed primarily toward the disposal of embarrassingly large agricultural surpluses, not toward the proper feeding of hungry families. It was for this reason, Agriculture officials argued, that the commodity distribution program delivered only surplus commodities whose total nutritional value was far below normal requirements, whose preparation and storage was difficult, and whose bulk often prohibited families lacking adequate transport from participating. It was for the same reason that the food stamp program, under which poor families bought stamps which could be used to purchase food worth more than the cost of the stamps, charged its participants more for stamps than most poor families could afford to pay, and gave in return stamps worth much less than the cost of a fully adequate diet.

Explaining food program failures on grounds that these programs were not directed toward providing the poor with good diets was an honest response to the initial discovery of hunger in Mississippi. Programs designed when malnutrition was not thought to be a serious problem could hardly be expected to deal effectively with that problem. Much less honest has been the continuing failure of the Agriculture Department and the rest of government to respond to growing evidence of severe malnutrition with programs specifically designed to deal with that problem.

The first page in what has become a scandalous record

of governmental defensiveness, delay, and general unwilling-
ness to respond to the demonstrated need of its constituents
was written in Mississippi shortly after the visit of the
Senate Subcommittee on Employment, Manpower and
Poverty. Checking on the findings of the Subcommittee,
Agriculture Department investigators confirmed that diets
of the poor in rural Mississippi were abysmal. But new
efforts to correct this situation were not part of their recommendations. Instead they editorialized that "low-income
households in this Mississippi Delta county (Washington
County) accommodate themselves to a diet which low-
income households elsewhere would reject. . . . It may be
that low-income families place less value on food than we
think."

Having satisfied themselves that the poor do not really
care about eating, the bureaucrats put a few minor patches
on their food programs and relaxed, in hopes that the furore
would subside. But early in 1968 the Citizens' Board of
Inquiry's sweeping indictment of Federal food programs,
and a report that the benefits of the national school lunch
program went overwhelmingly to middle- and upper-income
children, produced new demands for a more adequate
response from Washington.

The net result: one Congressman wrote county health
officers, men who were themselves an integral part of the
system under attack, to ask whether they knew personally of
anyone who was starving. Given their official positions and
the fact that the weakened victims of hunger almost in-
variably succumb to a normally nonfatal disease before
actually starving, most of the health officers gave the pre-
dictable response. "No," they said, "we know of no cases
of outright starvation." On this evidence the Congressman
informed his colleagues that hunger was not a serious problem in this country.

This "evidence," of course, was hardly sufficient to end the controversy. Spring of 1968 brought the powerful CBS documentary "Hunger in America." Again the response from Washington was pathetic. In petulant reply, Agriculture Secretary Freeman seized on the minute factual errors to condemn CBS for a "biased, one-sided, dishonest presentation of a serious national problem." Congress, ever concerned over the quality of television programming, asked for an FBI investigation to see whether the poor who told CBS they were hungry were telling the truth!

But with Martin Luther King dead, and the poor people about to march into Washington, it became increasingly obvious that a more serious reply to poor, hungry Americans was required. What followed, during the months of May to December, 1968, was a classic example of the paralysis of leadership in the face of insistent moral demand. The events of those months were traced by Elizabeth Drew in the *Atlantic Monthly,* in the finest report yet written on the politics of hunger:

First Attorney General Ramsey Clark, then the President himself asked the various government agencies to draw up a list of administrative actions—which would not cost money—which could alleviate some of the difficulties of the poor. . . . Agriculture, however, remained defensive. In the end, the Agriculture response consisted of promising to get a food program into each of the thousand counties—which the President had already done nine months earlier; making more commodities available for surplus distribution; regulations to improve the school lunch program; and improved food packages for infants and expectant mothers. Some Administration officials think the poor were not grateful enough.

As it happened, the major reason this response was so paltry was that the White House was preparing one on a far grander scale for the President himself to present, probably in the form of a special message to Congress. . . . The Budget Bureau squirreled away some money to go with the message. The thought was that it would be delivered around the time of "Solidarity Day," on June 19, when thousands of others were to come to Washington to join the poor in a climactic march.

A number of reasons have been offered for why the President's Solidarity Message was never delivered: the mail in the White House was overwhelmingly against the Poor People's Campaign, and Resurrection City was out of control; Abernathy's final speech was likely to carry a stinging denunciation of the war in Vietnam; and the House of Representatives was going to vote at last on the tax bill the following day, and any move at that point by the President to increase government spending might jeopardize the long-negotiated compromise. The most important reason, however, was that the President simply did not want to be in the position of appearing to "respond to pressure." More startling to many was that after the poor had left town and the tax bill had passed, he still declined to move. He was focusing on the budget cuts that had to be made, annoyed at Freeman for getting out in front of him on the issue, still concerned at appearing to respond to pressure, and convinced that now that some legislation was moving on the Hill, it would be unseemly for him, the President, to appear to be running to catch up.

In the very last days of the Congressional session, with the President about to make a routine request for additional funds for various agencies that had fallen short of funds, the machinery around the government—in the Agriculture Department, in the Budget Bureau, in his own staff—geared up once more for a presidential request for more funds for food stamps and a major statement on the issue. Instead, he simply requested the $90 million and in the closing rush Congress gave him $55 million. Wait, it was said, for his farewell message in 1969.*

In his farewell message, Lyndon Johnson did not mention hunger.

* Elizabeth Drew, "Going Hungry in America," *Atlantic Monthly*, December, 1968.

Early in 1969, as the Select Committee on Nutrition and Human Needs sought again to pick up the issue, we found Federal feeding programs virtually the same as they had been in 1967. Despite well-publicized tinkering, the past two years of study, pressure, and almost continuous pleas for relief had resulted neither in the reform of old programs nor in any significant new efforts to combat malnutrition. The commodity distribution program remained a surplus disposal effort. Even with an expanded food package, it still failed to provide enough food to meet minimum nutritional requirements. Facilities for distributing the food had not improved, participants still faced serious transport problems, and the program itself was shrinking. The food stamp program, theoretically a much more efficient way of meeting the food needs of the poor, still lacked the funds to do that job. Stamps still cost up to 50 percent of a poor family's total income and met as little as 50 percent of their minimum food needs. Most disturbing of all, over three of every four poor families received no family food assistance of any kind.

The year 1969 brought mixed progress. The effort to deal with the hunger problem has gained vital new support, but actual relief remains a promise, not a reality. The new support has come from three critical sources:

—In a poll published in the spring of 1969, public opinion was tested for the first time. Nearly 70 percent favored expanded government programs to provide food assistance to the poor.

—At about the same time, Senators from several key southern states spoke in favor of major food program reform for the first time.

—Finally, President Richard Nixon made a long overdue national commitment to "eliminate hunger in America itself for all time."

This new support has had several important results. Within the Nixon Administration, it provided the impetus for the President to send up a strengthened food stamp proposal for action by the Senate and the House; and it led him to convene, late in the fall, the first White House Conference on Nutrition, organized and presided over by the President's consultant on nutrition needs, Dr. Jean Mayer.

Perhaps most striking, this new support resulted in the strongest food stamp bill ever passed by the Senate. The Food Stamp Act of 1969 would more than double the available funds for the food stamp program, and would provide a vastly expanded program in every needy county by the end of 1970. If properly implemented, it should end poverty-related malnutrition within two years. But this legislation must first secure approval in the House, where it will face serious opposition from the conservative Agriculture Committee without the active support of the President, who prefers his own less expensive program. And in the meantime, the poor will again be asked to wait while legislators study, administrative agencies quarrel, and the affluent majority looks on with mild disapproval.

For the individual who believes that it is morally indefensible to permit a family to go hungry when their hunger can be so easily alleviated, the sorry record I have presented here poses a fundamental problem. Does the system which has given us this record deserve further support, or is it hopeless to expect that system to respond effectively to a moral issue?

In my opinion, the American political system is stacked against effective response to moral demands only because the American people have seldom insisted on such a response. Even when the question is one on which a moral solution is favored by the majority, that same majority has usually been willing to permit the sort of painfully slow political wrangling which has characterized our approach to hunger. I do not believe this approach is inevitable. When a problem is presented to the United States government in strictly moral terms, and when a solution, rather than a prolonged debate, is demanded by a majority, then I believe a solution will be forthcoming.

The development of the hunger issue to date points up two critical failures on the part of American "liberals." We have failed first by framing our arguments in such a way that near-poor, lower-middle-class citizens see government efforts against hunger not as a confirmation of ethical values which they themselves share, but as another costly giveaway which will only raise their already high taxes. Should this failure continue, it could end all hope of effective action against hunger. Ethnic whites, who have only recently escaped poverty themselves, have a more immediate understanding of the hunger problem than do most self-proclaimed champions of the poor. They are the most natural allies of the poor, and a political leader who is able to relate their needs for better housing, jobs, and police protection to the very similar problems of the poor and the black, could win their support for an all-out campaign against hunger.

A second important mistake has been our failure, as liberals, to accept the political consequences of the moral argument we have made. Too often liberal Senators and Representatives have gone into battle for their ideals ready to compromise them at the first sign of a fight. It is almost as if they feel that Saint John's prophecy in the seventh chapter of Revelation, "They shall hunger no more," absolves them of any responsibility to try to right these wrongs in the here and now. While it is fine to take what you can get on a strictly political issue, it is wrong to declare loudly that hunger is a moral outrage requiring immediate solution, knowing full well that you plan to accept ineffective compromises rather than solutions.

Some issues simply cannot be compromised. Hunger is one. Our political system is uncomfortable when faced with these issues, but it need not be paralyzed. The poor know that their children are hungry, and they seek help. A majority believes that they should have this help. While our government may always tend to "look at problems in terms of the workings of Washington, not in terms of the problem itself," it will look at the hunger problem if it is required to do so by the people. We can and must require this effort, for food which we may provide tomorrow cannot redeem the lives of children who starve today.

THE POLITICS
OF MORALITY

by Senator
BARRY GOLDWATER

BARRY GOLDWATER

Long a leading spokesman for political conservatism, Senator Barry Goldwater of Arizona has a constituency which far exceeds the population of his native state. First elected to the Senate in 1952, he resigned his seat in 1964 to become the Republican Presidential nominee. Reelected to the Senate in 1968, he now sits on the Armed Services and Aeronautical and Space Sciences Committees. A retired major general in the U.S. Air Force Reserves, he is also an amateur radio aficionado.

Senator Goldwater is a member of the Episcopal Church and has long been involved in lay activities. His numerous books include the best-selling *Conscience of a Conservative*, *Why Not Victory?*, *Where I Stand*, *The Face of Arizona*, *People and Places*, and *Down the Green and Colorado Rivers*. He has written articles for many leading periodicals.

The Politics of Morality

For some time I have been bemused and concerned by the notion—advanced by political writers, academicians, and not a few clergymen—that morality attaches itself in some mysterious way to particular legislative proposals or political issues. By these lights, certain political viewpoints or proposed laws are judged to be "moral," so that those who favor them are said to be acting morally, while those who oppose them—for whatever reason—are by implication guilty of moral turpitude.

In 1964 I was attacked by many clergymen, including some in my own church, for an alleged lack of moral consciousness in voting against the Civil Rights Act. They adopted the simplified argument that this legislation was long overdue to redress grievances against a minority group, and that every lawmaker had an obligation—even an ethical duty—to support this legislation. It did me no good to point out time and time again that my objection to the bill was not to its purpose but to its form. No consideration was given to the fact that as a man of conscience I had taken an oath of office wherein I swore to God to uphold the Constitution to the best of my ability.

The proponents of the 1964 Civil Rights Act were actually too emotional to credit a belief that any member of the United States Senate who was active in politics might feel a responsibility to his oath of office. Because I was a contender for the Presidency, it was naturally assumed that everything I did had a political motivation. Had this actually been the case, of course, I would have forgotten my pledge to uphold the Constitution and gone along with the prevailing sentiment which demanded approval of this legislation.

I felt then, and I feel now, that the Civil Rights Act of 1964 was unconstitutional. However, I fully recognize that this is merely my interpretation of the Constitution, and I am not about to say that Members of Congress who felt this act was in accord with the provisions of the Constitution were being in any way morally delinquent. I voted against this bill because I felt my oath to uphold the Constitution required such action. Others voted for it because they felt the legislation was needed and that it did no harm to our constitutional safeguards.

There have been more recent examples of this kind of attempt to imbue a political issue with morality in the abstract. We have seen so-called moral proposals to end the Vietnam war by immediate unilateral withdrawal, to oppose the nomination of a Supreme Court Justice who was on the "wrong" side of civil rights and labor issues, and to enlist the full weight of the Federal bureaucracy in a campaign against hunger. In each case, proponents of the measure try to suggest that the vote on the issue will somehow separate the moral sheep from the goats.

I disagree. My own belief is that morality in politics should be confined to individuals rather than issues. The example of the 1964 civil rights bill illustrates how dangerous it can be for anyone to arrogate to himself the authority to render moral judgments on public figures because of their support for or opposition to a particular policy, program, or piece of legislation.

The attempt to give a political issue absolute moral sanction is especially dangerous when it is done on behalf of the organized church. I have heard of clergymen who told their congregations about the deep concern Christ had for the poor—and then implied that anyone who opposed a particular piece of antipoverty legislation was guilty of being unchristian.

Another example is even more illustrative. A certain minister I read about told his congregation that if they wanted to be good Christians the thing to do would be to go out and work for the enactment of a model cities bill in the Congress. Now it seems to me that a good case could also be made in direct opposition to such a claim—but this too would not be right. For example, it might be argued that the adoption of a specific antipoverty, model cities or urban renewal bill would place an unreasonable burden on the backs of American taxpayers and especially on low-income wage earners. This being the case, why wouldn't it be reasonable for a clergyman to tell his congregation that unless they went out and worked for the defeat of these legislative proposals, they would be guilty of hurting those least able to pay higher taxes?

Often the incursion of organized religion into politics is based on the premise of mass guilt—the notion that whole groups of people are responsible for wrongs or injuries done to other groups of people in other times (slavery and segregation of Negroes is an oft-cited example). I question the whole premise of mass guilt. It seems to me that we must each be responsible for our own actions as individuals, not as members or descendants of a group. I believe that in the final analysis ethical concern and morality are the responsibility of each individual, and this includes the clergy.

By confusing moral imperatives with practical political judgments, the church risks losing its authority in precisely that area of spiritual guidance which it should most carefully preserve. To borrow a phrase from the Scriptures, it is entirely possible that, if Christ had been confronted with such choices, he would have said, "Render therefore unto Caesar the things which are Caesar's; and unto God the things which are God's" (Matthew 22:21, KJV).

There is another matter of morality in public affairs which is becoming more and more important and which causes me a great deal of concern. That is the problem involved when people choose to obey only such laws as they feel are morally right. It makes no difference to me if they say they are willing to accept the penalty involved in such a violation. To me this is not a valid excuse for flouting the rules and regulations promulgated by lawmakers in the interest of an ordered society for the majority of the population.

Laws—even bad ones—are adopted for a purpose. That purpose most often is tied up with the protection of a majority of the citizens. For example, when an existing law forbids a march or demonstration on a particular highway or street, this law did not have its origin in a desire to deny any particular group the privilege of expressing their feelings. Rather, such a law was intended to protect both the pedestrians engaged in any such march and the motorists using the highway. The whole idea of individual citizens or groups of citizens arrogating to themselves the privilege of deciding which laws they will obey and which laws they will disobey is not only wrong, but downright dangerous. The only proper way for such a group to proceed is to take their case to the proper governing body and get the law changed if they don't like what it provides.

The idea of following only those rules of which we approve, or obeying only those laws which meet our own particular idea of morality, has a name: anarchy. When enough people feel free to go against laws adopted by the majority for the good of the majority, then we are tampering with the very fabric of a free society with ordered justice. If we permit scofflaws to prevail, we will begin an unraveling of the fabric and hasten to the ultimate destruction of personal liberty. I believe the ethics invloved here make it incumbent on honest, responsible citizens to obey the law so long as it exists, regardless of how unjust or immoral they may believe its provisions to be.

And it is the duty of every public official, especially those elected to serve, to set an example rather than to encourage civil disobedience or even criminal disobedience in the name of do-goodism. Our officials must accept their special responsibility toward the maintenance of law. We have a government of laws, not of men. We must obey the law ourselves, and demand public officials who scrupulously support the basic tenets of our Republic. The ethics involved here are direct and straightforward. They demand obedience to the law.

Without obedience to the law, there can be no order in a society of men. And order is an absolutely essential cornerstone of civilization. It stands to reason that a disorderly society cannot survive. Throughout history there has never been a single instance of a society flourishing and progress being made in an atmosphere of disorder. Quite to the contrary, the past shows us very clearly that societies which became lawless died soon afterward. Disintegration of civilization begins when any individual or group succeeds in placing its own interests above the welfare of the majority of persons living in that society. When order flees a civilization, the law of the jungle takes over. When there is no ordered justice, there can only be survival of the fittest.

The appalling fact is that we have come so far along the road of mass disobedience that thoughtful men have found it necessary to remind us of these ancient and universal lessons. In recent months we have seen and heard more and more evidence of a planned course of lawlessness across broad sections of this country. In certain places the situation has gotten out of hand and threatened to destroy all law and order. In this situation the morality and ethics are clear enough to me: our elected officials and our national leaders must shoulder responsibility for defending the precepts of law and order.

It is the system itself that must be defended, and I hasten to point out that I do not mean to imply that everyone involved in this system is above reproach. There have been cases of police brutality. There have even been cases where men entrusted with the duty of law enforcement have contributed to the powers of lawlessness. But these are isolated cases and cannot be held up as an ethical or moral reason for doing away with all elements of law and order. It has become popular in recent years among certain groups to belabor policemen merely because they are policemen. Some elements of the so-called New Left in this country refer to any uniformed defender of the law as a "pig." This is the quintessence of unethical behavior. Similarly, I believe any public official, be he elected or appointed, can be held to account for encouraging blanket criticism of law and order or for supporting mass civil disobedience in the name of some temporary, liberal-supported social goal.

I must also say that it saddens me when I hear holier-than-thou spokesmen justifying defiance of this country's military selective service laws in the name of a higher morality which opposes the concept of war as a national policy. Here we have the typical oversimplification which is characteristic of both adolescents and so-called intellectuals. The contention is that killing is wrong; consequently, the Vietnam war which requires American servicemen to kill their Communist enemies is also wrong. These passionate pacifists seem to think they are the first persons in the recorded history of mankind to abhor war and regard the act of killing another human being as wrong. The youthful critics of our current Asian policy—and of all wars waged on behalf of freedom—do not object to making full use of the benefits which freedom affords them. They fully enjoy the right to live affluently, to speak freely and even to demonstrate against the established order. However, they cannot see the necessity of utilizing military strength and economic power to protect this freedom.

The morality of our commitment in Vietnam is tied to an American pledge to help defend the freedom and right to self-government of the people of South Vietnam. This policy, developed and advocated by several American Presidents over the course of two decades, has been judged correct both from the standpoint of our strategic national interests and the cause of freedom throughout the world. That determination is the official and binding one on this country as an honorable member of the family of nations.

If Senator Fulbright, Dr. Spock, and the chaplain of Yale University happen to believe that their moral judgment is superior to and outweighs that of the United States government, then let them try to change policy by acting through legal channels rather than encouraging widespread resistance against proper legal procedures. The ethical, the moral, the honorable course for men who oppose the war in Vietnam is to attempt to change our national policy through the constitutional and democratic process of elections. I believe that until they can make their viewpoint prevail as the majority feeling of the American people, they are ethically bound to support their nation and their fighting men in Vietnam.

What I have attempted to say here is that it is too easy for individual men to assume and arrogate to themselves a high-minded moral purpose to justify actions that actually run counter to the wishes of the overwhelming majority of our people. I think we have learned enough to know now that mass civil disobedience can quickly lead to mass criminal disobedience. And in that direction lies the unraveling of the precious fabric of majority rule in a society of ordered justice.

I have said that morality in politics should be related to individuals rather than to issues. Political leaders, and especially elected ones, have a particular responsibility to take this lesson to heart. In addition to their immediate responsibilities to the people whom they represent or for whom they act in the affairs of government, they have a clear moral duty to set a high example of ethical conduct for all citizens. To no other group of people has so much trust been given; therefore, the least they can do is to live and act in such a way as to inspire trust and confidence. It is in setting an example that I believe we elected officials have the greatest responsibility.

The integrity of Congress has been an important concern to an overwhelming majority of our national legislators from the very beginning. But the issues have changed. In 1838 the House of Representatives became bitterly exercised over the question of whether four of its members should be punished for participating in a duel in which one Congressman, Jonathan Cilley of Maine, was killed. Since the days of dueling, the explosive growth and diversification of our nation and the enormous load this has placed on our government have brought new problems. Lobbying has increased as special interest and pressure groups have multiplied with each new problem brought on by developing technology, economic growth and social change. The already high cost of maintaining an adequate political image while in office is increasing annually. Today's complex society gives even greater scope for potential conflicts of interest. All these things add to potential motivation and support for misconduct.

Sheer size is one of the most important contributing factors to the problem we are discussing. It is important to remember that when the first Congress convened less than two hundred years ago, there were only twenty-six Senators and sixty-six Members of the House. Today there are one hundred Senators and 435 Representatives. When George Washington took office as President, there were only five Cabinet departments: State, Treasury, War, Justice and the Post Office. What passed for the Department of Agriculture was created by President Lincoln in 1862; for some time it got along with a single employee, the commissioner, who did not even have a clerk. Today the Department of Agriculture has more than 120,000 employees. The Federal government in all its branches has nearly three million employees.

The growth of our Congress and government, of course, have merely reflected the growth of our population, which has more than doubled since 1910. This growth has greatly increased the work load of Members of Congress in their representative function. A House Member in the first Congress, which met in 1789, had fewer than 50,000 constituents. When the number of seats in the House was increased to 435 in 1910, a Member was expected to represent some 200,000 constituents. Today an average constituency is upward of 450,000 people. When you add to these figures the tremendous increase in the number of Federal agencies and programs with which a Member of Congress must deal on behalf of his constituents, you begin to get an idea of the vastly larger problem that Congressmen and Senators now have in representing their districts and states.

The increased size of our nation and its government, the growing complexity of their activities, and the mounting pressures that they occasion have led to new problems in the realm of public ethics, and have created a twilight zone of uncertainty as to just what does constitute questionable behavior in the operation of our political system. For one thing, wealth has become a sometimes critical factor in political effectiveness. A man who is not wealthy is bound to find it increasingly difficult today, not only to conduct a successful campaign for election to office, but also to operate that office at peak efficiency for his constituents under allowable government expenses. At the same time, money is now much easier to come by than it was in the days of the depression or the immediate postwar period. There are an increasing number of special interests that have their own reasons for wanting to curry favor with men and women in government or in the Congress who might be able to affect those interests. This is not to say that these parties are out to bribe Members of Congress or officials of the judiciary or the executive branch. But it is true that they are out to make as many friends as possible in these areas of influence—and one of the easiest ways to do it is to assist in the financing of a campaign for public office or to help provide the funds needed to run an office.

To illustrate the problems posed by the increased cost of operating an efficient and effective Congressional office, I should like to quote from a letter written to the Washington *Post* by Senator Robert Packwood of Oregon. In this explanation of a special fund being raised to defray expenses not covered by his official allowance, Senator Packwood states the problem as well as I have ever seen it argued:

Your editorial of June 2 commented on the fund being raised on my behalf to defray expenses not covered by my Senate office allowance. In my estimation, this is an unfortunate regression back to the rich man-poor man syndrome.

Let's put the salary of a Senator in perspective. From my annual $42,500 Senate salary, approximately $14,000 is paid in Federal income taxes, $2,500 goes for Oregon income taxes, and another $4,000 is taken in miscellaneous payroll deductions, including retirement and medical and life insurance. This means my effective Senate salary is roughly $22,000. I have no other source of income.

At a conservative and minimum estimate, my Senate office faces the following annual expenses for which there is no Government allowance: ten trips to Oregon above the six paid for by the Government at approximately $340 per trip—$3,400; travel expenses of an Oregon field man of approximately $6,000 a year; and my travel within the State of Oregon of approximately $6,000. Counting just these basic expenses this totals $15,400 a year.

All Senators have similar expenses. Arithmetic shows that they cannot be met from a Senator's salary alone. The needed additional funds can be obtained in four ways: (1) independent wealth; (2) a rich patron; (3) honorariums (which according to the recently filed Senate Reports can total as high as $5,000 for a single speech); and (4) an independent fund.

I am not independently wealthy, and I refuse even to attempt to find a rich patron. The remaining alternatives for meeting office expenses are honorariums and independent funds.

You indicate in your editorial that these nonreimbursable office expenses should either be paid by me personally, which I obviously cannot afford, or should not be incurred. To quote you, "Senator Packwood should forgo these expenses as he forgoes other luxuries beyond his means." . . . It does not seem to me that when my Oregon field man travels to an Oregon port to view a prospective harbor improvement or when I make an inspection of conditions of poverty on an Eastern Oregon Indian reservation, that these are luxuries.*

Senator Packwood's letter goes on to point out that former Senator Wayne Morse disclosed outside income of $47,000 during 1962, and showed office expenses totaling almost $60,000, noting that "the Senate appropriation does not begin to pay for my office." Senator Packwood continues:

My reference to Senator Morse does not imply criticism of him. He was able to meet his office expenses because of a sizable outside income, and nowhere can I find any criticism of this practice by the *Washington Post*. Are Oregon constituents now to be penalized because a man with no independent wealth has been elected to serve them in the U.S. Senate? I think not, and for this reason I elected to bring the problem into the open. Hence the establishment of the fund.

The fund organizers have four principal rules:

1. The fund will be handled and administered by an independent committee.

2. The fund will accept no contribution over $100. Contributions exceeding that amount have already been offered and the excess over $100 has been returned.

3. The name of every contributor, the amount of the contribution, and the expenditures of the fund will be filed with both the Secretary of the United States Senate and the Secretary of the State of Oregon, and will be available for public examination.

4. The fund will be audited.

I have outlined my reasons why additional funds are needed to serve my constituents 3,000 miles away. I believe this job can be accomplished through citizen participation. Certainly the *Washington Post* does not want a Senate in which a poor

* Washington *Post,* June 12, 1969.

Senator, by the fact of his financial limitations, is disadvantaged in serving his constituency.

I have the utmost sympathy for Senator Packwood's position in this matter. It would be extremely difficult, if not impossible, for a man without private resources to function efficiently and properly as a member of the Senate. It cost me in the neighborhood of $120,000 of my own private funds to function as a Senator for twelve years. I do not mean that I was forced to spend the money; I mean rather that it was my desire to spend it in order to provide my state and my country with the kind of service I feel they deserve.

We have looked at just a few of the new ethical problems brought on by the increased size and complexity of our society and government. Let us now try to put these problems in perspective, and see if there may be some practical solutions that will at least help us to define misconduct more sharply, if not do away with it.

In any serious attempt to apply the principles of Christian ethics to political practice, it is vitally important that we understand the nature of man as it truly exists. As a conservative, I believe man's nature is such that he will have his failures and character defects no matter how many laws are passed in the name of morality and no matter how many codes of ethics are devised for any group of men— whether they be public officials or any other special group.

There is no way to legislate or arrange for men in a particular position of responsibility to become forever noble. Being human, man's nature is such that no matter what kinds of laws and regulations and codes are adopted, he will always be assailed by the same temptations that have plagued men and women since the days of Adam and Eve. A few will always allow their greed and avarice to overrule their regard for duty and morality. Some will always let their selfishness overrule their fear or dislike of breaking the law. Some will go to almost any length, engage in almost any kind of nefarious activity, show almost every kind of disregard for the rights of others, if this is what is required to feather their own nests.

While it is true that in any group of men there will be a few who break moral standards or take them lightly, it nevertheless pains me deeply when I hear people express the belief that *all* Members of Congress are on the make, or are basically dishonest, or carry with them a high tendency toward larceny. Of course it takes only one highly publicized example of wrongdoing to spread the unjustified belief that all Members are a bunch of crooks. Such generalizations are not unusual, and they develop quite naturally from the attention and publicity and moralizing that attends any case of questionable conduct on the part of one or a few Members.

But let us put this question into a little perspective. There is no doubt in my mind that, if comparable statistics were available on the rate of malfeasance in Congress as against rates of similar acts in business, industry and the professions, the results on a proportionate basis would be clearly to the credit of the Congress. And it is important for the American people to understand that in a large degree the Congress of the United States is actually a reflection of our society as a whole. One branch of the Congress is named the House of Representatives precisely because its members are charged with the duty of representing the two hundred million Americans who make up our country.

We err if we assume that, merely because a man is prominent enough in his community to be chosen for political office, he must have some special claim on exemplary behavior. As his name implies, he is representative, in the sense of being typical, of the American people. This being the case, there will be some Members of Congress who are inclined to cut legal corners just as there are on the Main Streets of America. Some members will perhaps be greedy or bigoted or just plain mean. Again, this is a reflection of the various human elements that make up our society. If America can indeed be called a melting pot, the elected Members of Congress, in body assembled, can be called a reasonable reflection of that amalgamating process.

If there are going to be a few rotten apples in any barrel, then what difference should Christian ethics make? This is not a point which can be proved objectively. For me it is a matter of personal conviction as a Christian. I believe that a dedicated Christian, or a man dedicated to any truly religious concepts (for I know highly moral men who happen to be American Indians, Muslims, Buddhists, etc.), will be better able to withstand the temptations that might come his way in public life than a person with no belief and little regard for moral values. To a man without religious convictions, the only reasons for being moral are practical ones—fear of disapproval or of being caught, inconvenience, psychological guilt. But a Christian, whether in politics or any other profession, practices morality not merely because of external sanctions but because of internal conviction. In his heart he knows he is either right or wrong, and this knowledge acts as a powerful incentive to proper conduct.

The question arises, Is it possible to conduct an investigation which would prove a man's moral worth prior to his election or appointment to an office of public trust? If it could be done, this would be the best insurance that could be devised for the maintenance of a higher ethical standard in the ranks of our public servants. But to date no one has seriously suggested that such a test is possible. We can measure behavior when it is possible to observe it, but many of a man's actions are as private as his conscience, and his thoughts and motives are even further hidden from public view. I am reminded of Proverbs 23:7, "As he thinketh in his heart, so is he" (KJV). Furthermore, it is often difficult to predict whether a man who has always been known for honesty and fairness in his dealings with others will continue to resist temptation once he is subjected to the pressures of public office. As Lord Acton said, "Power corrupts, and absolute power corrupts absolutely."

While there is considerable evidence that the ethical standards of Congress are higher today than they have ever been, a few highly publicized recent examples of wrongdoing have led the legislative branch to give increasing attention to methods of avoiding such incidents. Indicative of the growing demand for Congressional action is the number of proposals relating to standards of official conduct introduced in the Congress in recent years. In the eleven-year period from 1957 to 1967, some 336 such measures were sponsored in the House and forty-three in the Senate. All were designed to provide enforceable standards of conduct for Members and employees of the Congress. Except for statutes on bribery, corruption and other criminal offenses, the existing laws provided for almost no enforcement machinery.

The new attention led both the House and the Senate to create committees to study the subject and make recommendations. Both committees made their recommendations in March, 1968, and as a result both Houses of Congress adopted codes of conduct plus requirements for annual reports of outside financial interests. Both Houses now have continuing committees to monitor the conduct of their respective members and employees. It is important to note that these committees have investigative and enforcement powers, but their recommendations in any given case— whether for reprimand, censure, expulsion or other disposition—are subject to the action of the Senate or the House.

Congress has always had power under the Constitution to discipline its members. But the feeling was growing that there had long been a need for specific guidelines of conduct. In and of itself a code of ethics will obviously not provide an easy solution for any problems that might arise. But I do feel that it will be helpful if some kind of direction is provided in uncharted areas of questionable official conduct. I further believe that the adoption of these guidelines will be beneficial in helping to provide the public with the correct image of the nation's lawmakers.

As a Senator, I am naturally more concerned with the Senate Code (see Appendix I). It takes the form of an amendment to the Standing Rules of the Senate, incorporating four new rules covering (1) outside business or professional activity or employment by officers or employees, (2) contributions, (3) political fund activity by officers and employees, and (4) disclosure of financial interests. The intent of the first new rule is to help Senators and their employees avoid any conflicts of interest that might arise from professional interests or loyalties outside the Senate. The major purpose of the other three rules is to make public the sources and uses of monies received by Senators and/or their employees, thus bringing implicit sanction against any illegitimate or questionable receipts and disbursements.

The new Senate rules require full disclosure of the financial affairs of Members and employees of the Senate who are compensated at a rate in excess of $15,000 a year. Conflict of interest occurs when a Member's personal financial holdings might be affected by the passage of a certain piece of legislation. For example, let us say that a Member of the Senate owns or controls a television or radio station. Any legislation coming before the Senate that might affect the regulation of these stations, or that might govern actions of the Federal Communications Commission which watches over this industry, would have a bearing of some kind on this Member's business. I am not suggesting that any man who has such an interest is going to be governed entirely by his personal involvement in any vote he might cast. I believe it is possible for a Member to act objectively or even to vote against his own best interests on legislation of this kind—but we cannot be sure of this. I believe it is honorable and preferable for any Member having a large personal stake in any piece of legislation coming before the body in which he serves to excuse himself from the deliberations and the decision. And to encourage him to avoid this kind of conflict of interest, the financial disclosure for which the Senate rules now provide make it apparent what that Member's personal interest might be.

Naturally this whole process gets back to what I discussed in the beginning: the question of personal honesty. The most effective code for preventing dishonest conduct is an internal one. However, if we accept the frailties in human nature and wish to guard against undue conflict of interest in legislative matters, I believe the Senate resolution should be much broader than the one mentioned above. For example, the Senate resolution says nothing about interests held by a Member's brothers or sons or cousins. In other words, it requires disclosure only of the interests held by the Member, and by the Member's wife if their interests are jointly held. However, if a Member's wife has large specific interests which are not held jointly with her husband, then this gives the Member a family stake, if not a direct personal stake, in the adoption or rejection of legislation which might affect those interests. The same type of situation would pertain to a Senator whose brother might be one of the nation's largest bankers or manufacturers. Legislation affecting the banking or manufacturing industry in which the brother is involved certainly could have an indirect effect on the way a Member considered a piece of pending legislation. I am not about to suggest that any such complete disclosure of interests held by a Member's relatives is a simple or even a feasible matter. I merely point it out to show that the best of resolutions adopted after long and careful consideration will still have loopholes through which potential conflicts of interest can easily slip. To come really to grips with such conflicts of interest, I believe disclosure should go much further than is presently required.

Only time will tell whether the new codes of ethics adopted by the House and Senate will have a salutary effect on the behavior of Members who might otherwise be tempted to use their public office for the pursuit of personal gain. Will the House of Representatives become collectively more honest because it has adopted a code of official conduct? Will the Senate of the United States become overnight a bastion of honesty and integrity because it has adopted a code of standards? Will the Federal judiciary be removed from all suggestion of impropriety because a code of ethics was adopted under the auspices of former Chief Justice Earl Warren?

The Washington *Daily News,* in an editorial dated May 30, 1969, raised the question of just how effective such codes can be. Noting that Justice William O. Douglas received $350 from publisher Ralph Ginzburg for an article in the March issue of Ginzburg's off-beat magazine, *Avant Garde,* the editorial went on to say:

> By taking this fee from a man who has been convicted of mailing obscene matter and whose case has been before the Supreme Court and could come up again, Justice Douglas clearly trespassed on the canon which requires a judge not only to be free from impropriety but from the appearance of impropriety.
>
> At the least, this fee taking was a reckless if not arrogant disregard not only of the legal profession's canons but of ordinary standards of conduct from one in so exalted a position.
>
> But if the canon of his own profession would not deter Justice Douglas, either in taking a salary from a foundation (from which he only recently resigned under pressure) or in selling an article to a convicted pornographer, what effect would another "code of conduct" have?

What the newspaper was saying, and what I have been trying to underscore, is that while a decent understanding of ethics ought to be a primary qualification for any public official, yet if he does not have that understanding instinctively and naturally, then a code will be only a minor help to him.

Given the limitations of human nature, no code of ethics will be a panacea. The new House and Senate Codes should help to define areas of questionable conduct, so that no Member may claim ignorance of the standard against which his behavior is to be measured, and in this respect they represent a significant step forward. But the only real assurance of good conduct in Congress, on the bench, or in the executive branch of government lies in the conscience of the men who hold these positions.

For in the final analysis, if elected officials will not keep faith with the public, then the public will withdraw the trust that has been vested in them. The traditional penalty for betrayal of public trust is eviction from office. Whenever public immorality becomes blatant and inexcusable, the rallying cry of the reformers will always be heard: "Throw the rascals out!" Thus the final jury is the public itself, and from this point a simple fact derives: the ultimate custodian of political morality is the people themselves, and conduct which is daily countenanced by the average citizen will not be eschewed by his elected representatives. Thus Saul, first king of Israel, fell into dishonor because the people of Israel dishonored the Lord in asking Samuel to give them a king. And thus today a politician who sees canons of ethics everywhere ignored will feel no special responsibility to conform to standards that his constituents themselves do not appear to take seriously. A righteous people will demand, and get, moral leadership. If the American people do not get moral leadership from their elected officials, then I submit that we must look to our own hearts as well as to codes of conduct for the answer.

CONGRESSIONAL ETHICS

☆ ☆

by Congressman
CHARLES E. BENNETT

CHARLES E. BENNETT

In 1966 Congressman Charles E. Bennett of Florida was named chairman of the first Ethics Committee in the history of the United States House of Representatives. He has been the Democratic Representative from Jacksonville since 1949, and has not missed a roll-call vote in the House since 1951. A senior member of the House Armed Services Committee, he has authored legislation establishing the first permanent Ethics Committee in the House, the national motto "In God We Trust," a loyalty oath for government employees, a code of ethics for government service, and the People to People program.

An active Protestant layman, Congressman Bennett is an elder in the Riverside Christian Church of Jacksonville. He is the author of *Laudonnière and Fort Caroline* and *Settlement of Florida,* in addition to articles in several leading journals.

Congressional Ethics

A nation, it has been said, has no morals except as its individual citizens have morals. It could as well be said that an institution like the United States Congress has no morals except as its Members conform to the highest standards of personal conduct.

In the last few years the Congress has been rocked by disclosures of unethical behavior and breaches of public trust by Members of the House and Senate. Public-opinion polls have revealed that most Americans believe many Congressmen to be corrupt, and the foundations of the 180-year-old institution have been shaken by mounting public criticism. By any standards, the growing list of misconduct cases should be cause for public concern:

• In 1940 a Georgia Congressman was indicted on charges of conspiring to barter and sell appointive offices.

• An investigating committee of the Senate in 1946 found that a Mississippi Senator had "improperly used his high office . . . for personal gain" in helping two war contractors.

• A year later a Representative from Kentucky was convicted of taking money to influence the award of War Department and other agency contracts to a munitions firm.

• In 1949 a New Jersey Congressman pleaded no contest

to charges of payroll padding and receiving salary kick-backs.

- Two Congressmen, one in 1956 and one in 1958, were indicted for income-tax evasion.
- Two more Congressmen were convicted on charges of conspiracy and conflict of interest in 1963.
- The Senate found one of its officers guilty of "gross improprieties" in 1964.
- A Connecticut Senator in 1967 was censured for using political testimonial funds for his private and personal benefit.
- In the same year a New York Congressman was found guilty of maintaining his wife on his office payroll when she performed no actual duties, of improper expenditure of public funds for personal use, and of conduct "unworthy of a Member." His colleagues denied him his seat and fined him for bringing discredit upon the House of Representatives.

A Gallup poll taken shortly after this last incident reported that 60 percent of those polled believed the misuse of government funds by Congressmen is fairly common. Public confidence in the Congress had been shaken to its roots, and the growing ire of taxpayers served to spur needed reforms within the Congress, including a set of standards to guide our lawmakers.

Things are not, I believe, as bad as the Gallup poll suggested. Almost eleven thousand men and women have served in the United States Senate and House of Representatives since their beginnings in 1789. Of that number only seventy-three—or ½ of 1 percent—have ever been expelled, censured, or excluded from service. The incidence of actual corruption in Congress is miniscule, but this does not excuse the exceptions or eliminate the need for ethical reform and well-defined codes of standards for

Members. The pressures and problems Congressmen face are enormous, and if our most prestigious representative institution is to be kept free of the taint of corruption and scandal, then Senators and Congressmen should be given clear guidelines as to the level of conduct expected of them by the public.

Congress, of course, is not the only branch of the Federal government that has been touched with scandal in recent years. Glaring breaches of public trust have been disclosed in the executive and judicial branches as well. In 1958 a Presidential assistant resigned after being criticized for accepting gifts from a businessman under investigation for improper activities. A Presidential military aide was widely censured for accepting a food freezer from a friend he had helped in Europe. A member of the Federal Communications Commission resigned under pressure because of his ties to television-station applicants. And recently a Supreme Court Justice bowed out of office following disclosure of his ties to a foundation controlled by a convicted investor.

Though instances of misconduct can be found at every level and in all branches of government, it is Congressmen and Senators—perhaps because they are supposed to be the people's closest link to the Federal government—who are watched most closely for breaches of ethics. In his inimitable way Mark Twain once heaped disapprobation on Members of Congress, likening them to the most devious of birds:

You may call a jay a bird. Well, so he is in a measure—because he's got feathers on him, and don't belong to no church, perhaps; but otherwise he is just as much a human as you be. And I'll tell you why. A jay's gifts, and instincts, and feelings, and interests, cover the whole ground. A jay hasn't got any more principle than a Congressman. A jay will lie, a jay will steal, a jay will deceive, a jay will betray; and four times out of five a jay will go back on his solemnest promise.

It is a good thing Mark Twain is known as a humorist, or there would be a lot more people who might take him seriously, and the turnover on Capitol Hill would be much, much greater.

Senators and Representatives daily face questions which could involve conflict of interest, nepotism, misuse of funds, improprieties over campaign funding, lobbying, junkets and gifts, or other breaches of ethical behavior. The incidence of misconduct, the moral problems facing an elected representative, and the cures are basic questions for discussion in a volume on Christian ethics and political practice.

Public ethics have been of great personal concern to me since the beginning of my public career. In fact this was one of the factors which first led me into politics. It was my childhood goal to run for political office and serve in public life, and several things encouraged me in this dream.

At the age of six I visited President Woodrow Wilson in the White House. My father was a United States weatherman at the time, and he took me with him to see the President. It was an age when private citizens could very freely visit the President, whereas today only a handful of our two hundred million citizens ever have this personal privilege. The visit to the White House became a lasting inspiration to me, and it was one factor in my later running for office.

When I was growing up in Tampa, Florida, during the 1920's, the city government was corrupt and despotic. Former United Press President Karl Bickel called Tampa "a city without a soul." Virgil M. Newton, Jr., former editor of the crusading Tampa *Tribune,* wrote:

In 1928 this politically inspired municipality kicked out the city manager form of government and, through political chicanery, installed the aldermanic ward system, which autocratically ruled the city for the next 17 years. Under this ward system, the mayor was elected city-wide; the twelve aldermen were chosen one from each of the 12 wards. Seven of the twelve aldermen organized into a majority bloc with the shrewdest alderman as chairman of the board. The seven majority-bloc aldermen were elected by a combined total of only 5623 votes in their seven wards. This represented less than 20 percent of the registered city vote and about four percent of Tampa's official population. In other words, some five thousand voters, many of them feeding on special privilege, governed the remaining 120,000 through a despotic majority bloc of ward heelers.

In this atmosphere little was accomplished in Tampa. Taxes kept rising. Raw sewage was dumped into Tampa Bay, the beauty spot of Florida's West Coast. City streets cracked and crumbled, and public buildings were allowed to deteriorate. Political appointees flooded city offices. The police force was inadequate and in large part corrupt. Crime continued to increase; a strong organized-crime racket developed. Illegal gambling and prostitution were protected; narcotics traffic flourished. It was as if Tampa was daring anyone to find her soul.

Fortunately for Tampa, in 1945 the Tampa *Tribune* accepted the challenge and launched a full-fledged campaign against the old, corrupt city government. From that date, the city began to prosper and flourish, and Tampa now prides itself on one of the most modern and efficient city governments in the country.

My concern for morality was stimulated finally by my parents' dedication to the principles of our denomination, the Disciples of Christ:

No creed but Christ, no book but the Bible, no name but the divine.
Where the Scriptures speak, we speak; where the Scriptures are silent, we are silent.
In essentials, unity; in opinion, liberty; and in all things, charity.
We are not the only Christians, but Christians only.

My mother and father also left me a legacy of concern for independence and individualism, two pillars of Christian doctrine which I believe are essential prerequisites for an ethical political leader in our democratic system. Perhaps most important, they encouraged a lasting commitment to personal honesty.

Honesty is the fundamental attribute demanded by the electorate, and in my view it should be the primary characteristic of the politician. Yet few things are more difficult to define. The law may be written down in black and white, but personal integrity is not subject to clear definition: it is a gray area where moral principles must be applied in confusing situations which are not spelled out in rule book or text. Laws can punish us for being bad, but they cannot make us good. We draw our deepest convictions not from laws or books but from other human beings—our family, our church, our friends, the society in which we live.

Morality evolves from the hearts and minds of men, and like the tracings left by fingertips on wet sand, it can be washed away in the sweep of the tide. Individual integrity, forged with such difficulty, can be destroyed with seeming ease. Even moral giants crack under the tremendous pressure of divided loyalties—to party, friends, campaign contributors, family. An elected representative can easily violate, without intending to, the spirit of Christ's teaching in the Sermon on the Mount: "No man can serve two masters."

While morality is thus a matter of individual conscience and judgment, all men are mutually responsible to each other for moral behavior in difficult situations. One man's decision, especially if he is a public leader, may have a profound impact upon the whole government and society. This realization was one of the important factors in my early decision to seek public office.

The visit to President Wilson, my family training, and the experience of growing up in a city dominated by the very worst type of politics whetted my interest in public life. I saw the potential influence of politicians for good or evil, and I determined to lead a personal and political life that would be as exemplary as possible. These early experiences are also the root of my continuing interest in improving standards of conduct among public officials. I have tried to live Theodore Roosevelt's admonition: "To educate a man in mind and not in morals is to educate a menace to society."

Philosophers and kings have wrestled with problems of public morality since the beginning of recorded history. In the chamber of the House of Representatives, twenty-three of the world's great lawgivers have been immortalized in bas-relief marble portraits. Here is Hammurabi, king of Babylonia, who twenty centuries before Christ gave man his first written code of ethics. Hammurabi's Code covered the whole range of human behavior, from marriage to criminal law and the law of torts, but high on his list were admonitions against offering bribes and warnings against improper behavior by government officials.

Several hundred years after Hammurabi, Moses delivered to the Children of Israel the divinely given Ten Commandments, the best-known, but not always the best-followed, code of law in the history of the Judeo-Christian tradition. Christian statesmen from Constantine the Great to John Calvin and Abraham Lincoln have been guided by its precepts, and it remains a touchstone for the Christian legislator today.

Not so well known is the great lawgiver of ancient Sparta, Lycurgus, who lived a thousand years before Christ. Lycurgus counseled against having any of his laws put in writing. He felt that if a country is to be happy and virtuous, its law should be printed in the hearts of its citizens. He wrote that love and goodwill are far stronger ties than any compulsory law, "which when men by use and custom through good education do take in their childhood, it maketh every man to be a law to himself."

The laws of Lycurgus, "written in the heart," are an ideal. But few men have been able to live up to such an ideal, and over the centuries great lawgivers have relied on religion, written law, and the balance of institutions to check man's natural impulse to aggrandize his own interests at the expense of other weaker men. The history of the development of our own representative form of government is a classic illustration of this process.

The roots of American representative government go back to the controversy and conflict of sixteenth-century Europe. It was a time of political machination, social turmoil, religious war and persecution, mass executions and reigns of terror. Tyrant kings ruled by what they called divine right. The Duke of Alva persecuted Protestants in the Netherlands. Czar Ivan the Terrible executed hundreds accused of a plot to kill the Russian crown prince. Mary Queen of Scots was beheaded for treason. And Catherine de Medici, Queen Mother of France, resorted to mass murder to accomplish her political aims: she instigated the St. Bartholomew's Day Massacre of 1572, a crime which earned for her not only a unified nation but the blessings of the Pope.

Catherine and other rulers of this period drew much of their inspiration from Niccolò Machiavelli, author of *The Prince,* a Renaissance ruler's guide to the judicious use of deception, intrigue, treachery, force and fear. Machiavelli believed that social order depended on some sort of supernatural belief; accordingly he wrote that a ruler should support religion and appear to be religious, whatever his private beliefs. But he rejected the ethic of Christianity—its conception of goodness as gentleness, humility, nonviolence, its love of peace and denunciation of war, its assumption that states, as well as citizens, are bound by one moral code. To Machiavelli, morality was a code of conduct by which the state maintained collective order; hence the ruler would fail in his duty if, in defending the state, he should allow himself to be restricted by the same moral code that supposedly bound his citizens. Similarly, a diplomat should not feel bound by the moral code of his own people: "When the act accuses him, the result should excuse him." The end justified the means.

Thus the authority of these sixteenth-century European rulers, derived from what they called divine right, was exercised through deception, terror, and immorality. Europe's kings and queens practiced Machiavellian rule not only abroad but at home as well. Religious and political turmoil swept across the continent, through France and Spain, England and the Netherlands, in the sixteenth and seventeenth centuries. The exploration and colonization of the New World were spurred in large measure by the upheavals and persecutions which threatened to engulf the Old.

The men who settled America in this early period were fleeing two kinds of tyranny, political and religious. Many felt that the greatest threat to political freedom lay in the institution of the monarchy itself. "A monarchy," observed Alexander Campbell, founder of the Disciples of Christ Church, "is the cheapest, most efficient, and the most dignified [form of government]; provided only that the crown is placed on the wisest head, and the sceptre wielded by the purest hands. Could we always secure this, we would all be monarchists; because we cannot, we are all republicans." In our century Reinhold Niebuhr has echoed the thought: "Man's capacity for justice makes democracy possible, but man's inclination to injustice makes democracy necessary."

The early English colonists had ready at hand a model for representative government—the English Parliament. Shortly after the founding of Jamestown, Virginia, in 1607, its settlers elected representatives to the newly established House of Burgesses, the oldest organ of democratic government in our American history, and one which set a precedent for all future self-rule in the colonies. A few years after the founding of Jamestown, Puritan Separatists from the Church of England landed at Plymouth, Massachusetts. On shipboard they had signed the Mayflower Compact, an agreement to form a local representative government and abide by laws based on their religious heritage.

When the time came to write a new constitution for the newly independent United States in the 1780's, our Founding Fathers already had a rich legacy on which to draw for inspiration. The French philosopher Montesquieu had provided the doctrine of the separation of powers: each branch of government checks and balances the other; there is a division of power; justice is secured and the natural rights of men are preserved. The English system as it had developed in the eighteenth century provided the working model for a new government of three branches—the executive, the judiciary, and the two-house legislative branch.

To most of these first settlers, religious freedom was as important as political liberty. Fort Caroline in Florida was the first settlement within the confines of the United States to emphasize man's right to worship God in freedom. The French colony founded by René Laudonnière in 1564 set a precedent followed by Rhode Island under Roger Williams. Shortly before the American Revolution, Thomas Jefferson wrote a guarantee of absolute religious freedom into the laws of Virginia, and that act became a model for the framers of the Constitution.

Yet while they valued religious liberty, the early colonists and founders of our nation realized that many of society's deepest values have their origins in religion. They would have agreed with Edmund Burke, the great English conservative, who wrote: "We know and we feel inwardly that religion is the basis of civil society, and the source of all good and all comfort."

The Latin word *religare,* from which "religion" is derived, means "to tie back, tie up and tie fast" that which has been broken away or dissolved. As religious beings we believe that we must obey certain basic principles, without which society would be a shambles. As Alexander Campbell put it, "The works of God and the words of God, or the things done or spoken by God, are those facts which are laid down and exhibited in the Bible as the foundation of all faith, hope, love, piety, and humanity."

Our Republic has flourished because the men who have led the nation have respected religion and insisted on religious freedom. Throughout four hundred years of settlement and almost two hundred of nationhood, we have found that harmony in government has been best achieved when based on strong religious principles. This concern has led, I believe, to order in our society, to justice in the laws passed by our councils and legislatures, and to freedom for our people. Democratic government has not given us religion, law, and ethics—rather religion, law, and strong moral standards have produced a workable republic, our democratic system.

While we acknowledge our debt to religion and to our sophisticated legal system, our ethical behavior as private and public men is subject to change at a much faster pace than religion or law. Though we could not say Catherine de Medici had no religion and was not obeying her own laws at the time of the wholesale massacres in France, we can and do question the ethics of her behavior. She adapted her moral standards to suit herself. But public morality has improved considerably since Catherine's day. Her machinations to us in the twentieth century would seem not just crude but monstrously immoral.

The moral standards that people expect their rulers to keep *do* change, and significant progress has been made through the institutions of representative democracy. But there are still gray areas where no laws or standards of conduct govern the behavior of public officials, and I believe that so long as personal integrity, rather than strict adherence to written laws, is the measure of morality—for so long will Senators and Representatives and all other elected officials face questions of right and wrong to which there are no easy answers. Among those areas where today's Congressmen are most in need of guidelines are questions involving the financing of campaigns, lobbying and personal gifts, conflict of interest cases, nepotism, and junketing.

"Politics has got so expensive it takes a lot of money even to get beat with," Will Rogers said not many years ago. In the 1968 Presidential election the two major parties spent a reported total of $50 million, while the third-party candidate, George Wallace, spent some $8 million. This did not include contests for 435 seats in the House of Representatives, thirty-four Senatorial seats, twenty-one governorships, or local races. To run a statewide campaign in Florida today costs a million dollars, and some Congressional candidates spend over $100,000 to be elected—or defeated! The costs of running for office are already exorbitant and still mounting, and this pressure can easily lead candidates to resort to secret or questionable campaign funding.

The problem is not a new one. At the beginning of this century Theodore Roosevelt recommended that Congress provide "an appropriation for the proper and legitimate expenses of each of the great national parties." During the 1920 Presidential campaign, a Democratic candidate, William Gibbs McAdoo, said: "If the national government paid the expenses of the national campaigns and specified the legitimate objects for which expenditures might be made, politics would be purified enormously."

It is media expenses that have sent the basic cost of waging a campaign skyrocketing in all parts of the country.

There have been many suggestions for holding down these expenditures: radio and television time and newspaper and magazine space might be given free to candidates as a public service, or the funds spent in these areas held to a statutory minimum. A 1967 Gallup poll reported that 73 percent of the public favored a limit on campaign spending.

The present system of Federal reporting of campaign funds is ridiculous: it allows candidates for Congress to avoid reporting any campaign contributions or expenditures at all through the use of committees, which are not required to report. The Federal Corrupt Practices Act of 1925 stipulates that a candidate for U.S. Senator can spend only $25,000 on his campaign, a U.S. Representative only $5,000. A Massachusetts Senator was said to have spent over $2 million to be elected in 1962, but because a committee handled his finances, he reported to the Congress that his campaign expenses were zero.

Methods of raising political funds are varied: direct contributions; the loan of material items such as automobiles, airplanes or office space; payment of expenses through a law firm or public-relations agency; and dinners. More and more politicians are using the dinner vehicle, and the cost of filet mignon has jumped from a $100-a-plate donation only five years ago to $1,000 for Republicans and $500 for Democrats in 1970.

There should be no evil implication attached to collecting funds from the general public for the financing of legitimate political expenses. But the public has the right to know who is contributing to their elected officials and in what amounts, just as in the case of campaign contributions. Otherwise the public cannot pass judgment intelligently on possible conflicts of interest.

Public disclosure may be the best answer to these problems of private political financing. Disclosure would attach no moral overtones to the financial situation of a particular member or candidate. But it would make the public the final arbiter in any controversy over political funding. All facts and figures would be available to the people, who would decide at the polls whether an elected official has been guilty of improper behavior. As public office is a public trust, each elected official should be responsible for public disclosure of his outside sources of finance.

The House and Senate have limited disclosure provisions at the present time. A much stronger law is needed. Legislation which I first introduced in the Ninetieth Congress would establish the House Financial Disclosure Act, calling for a full public accounting by representatives and candidates for the House of Representatives. The bill would require a complete breakdown of income, assets, gifts and liabilities, as well as a description of all slush funds maintained by a member or candidate for expenses not connected with elections. I have also introduced a bill requiring a code of ethics and disclosure for Federal judges.

Directly related to political financing is lobbying, a much-misunderstood process. Sometimes abused and often carrying a bad connotation, lobbying is nevertheless a vital part of the daily interchange between the people and their government. Put simply, it is the representation of a group's interests before governmental bodies.

The term "lobbying" comes from newspaper shorthand in the 1820's for persons who frequented the lobbies of government buildings in order to speak to legislators or officials. By 1852 the practice had become bothersome enough that the House forbade access to the floor to newspapermen employed as agents to talk up any bill pending before Congress. Two years later the House established a select committee to investigate the efforts of Samuel Colt, the gun manufacturer, to secure extensions of a patent; Colt had allegedly used bribes and other illegal means to influence a House vote on a particular bill.

Despite several investigations of lobbying in Congress, the first general law was not passed until 1946, when the Federal Lobbying Act was included as part of the Legislative Reorganization Act. The law requires anyone who solicits or receives funds for the purpose of lobbying Congress to register with the clerk of the House and the secretary of the Senate, and to file quarterly financial reports. It does not restrict the activity of lobbyists, nor is the reporting system policed.

In my view, public-disclosure regulations are needed to ensure that only proper lobbying is done. For several years I have sponsored lobbying legislation which would require policing by the Comptroller General, who would be empowered to prescribe stronger methods of reporting the activities of lobbyists, to ascertain if accurate reports are filed by all lobbyists, and to refer any violations of the law to the Justice Department for appropriate action. I feel this bill would dispel the mysteries of lobbying and help to keep the legislative process honest and open. As the 1951 Senate Report, "Ethical Standards in Government," says, disclosure would act like an antibiotic to attack "ethical sickness" in public affairs.

Bribes, invitations, and gifts are hardest to deal with when they are directed toward personal influence rather than specific legislation. Public officials live in an atmosphere of unending invitations and gifts, not all of which are intended to win improper influence. Like other men, Congressmen and Senators are stimulated by different things—liquor, sex, money, power—and some are weaker and fall prey more easily than others to the influence of these attractions.

Honoraria for making speeches or writing articles for lobbying groups provide side incomes for Congressmen. Some Senators and Representatives can make $3,000 for a single luncheon speaking engagement. Scores of Congressmen participate in these activities although there is doubt about the propriety of some of these engagements.

Where to draw the line is an agonizing question for many elected officials. Former Senator Paul Douglas of Illinois used to say he would accept no gifts worth more than $2.50. Others say they will accept nothing that cannot be consumed in one day, or one hour. My own rule is not to accept any gifts except from my immediate family. Perishable citrus from Florida, peanuts from Georgia and cranberries from Washington are delivered to my door every year. They are then sent to one of the military hospitals in the Washington, D.C., area, after the donor is notified that this is being done because of my rule against taking gifts. Other gifts of value go back to the giver. This is painful, especially when a gift comes from an old and dear friend, but it is a rule.

There are more flagrant violations of ethics than taking a gift, or being treated to a fine dinner, or spending the weekend at a lobbyist's expense, but the line must be drawn by each elected official in the absence of a strict regulation or law. One of the worst payoffs for favoritism by a government official is not a gift or a meal, but a lucrative job on the outside. In 1951 I introduced a bill which prohibited for two years the employment of a former Federal government employee by any concern with which certain kinds of transactions were handled. The objectives of this bill were written into the Federal Conflict of Interests Law adopted in 1962. I have introduced a stronger bill recently in light of the disclosure that over 2,000 former military officers (Army colonels, Navy captains, and above) are now employed by the one hundred largest corporations in America.

Many of the most perplexing ethical questions with which Congressmen and Senators have to deal fall under the broad heading of "conflict of interests."

In the 1830's an historic battle took place in Washington between Senate supporters of the Second Bank of the United States, which was seeking renewal of its charter, and President Andrew Jackson, who opposed renewal. Among the bank's defenders on the Senate floor was the black-browed and imperious Daniel Webster of Massachusetts, a great orator and formidable champion of the financial interests represented by the bank. He had been privately retained by the bank to act on its behalf, while at the same time, of course, he was supposed to be representing the public as Senator from Massachusetts.

As the bank struggle reached its climax late in 1833, Webster wrote to Nicholas Biddle, president of the bank, as follows: "Sir: Since I have arrived here I have had an application against the Bank, which I have declined of course, although I believe my retainer has not been renewed, or refreshed as usual. If it be wished that my relation to the Bank should be continued, it may be well to send the usual retainers." This bit of open directness worked and the retainer was "refreshed." Thomas Carlyle, the Scottish essayist who once said that no man could be as great as Daniel Webster seemed to be, might have been a little dismayed.

In 1969, the first reporting by the House Ethics Committee disclosed that twelve of thirty-five members in the House Banking and Currency Committee owned stock in financial institutions. *The Wall Street Journal* revealed that one member of this committee owed $155,000 to four banks in New York and Florida.

It is especially difficult in conflict-of-interest cases to set guidelines that are both clear and realistic. Plato suggested that members of the ruling class should have no personal economic interests whatsoever outside their limited government compensation. Thomas Jefferson, in his manual of parliamentary practice, was equally emphatic: "Where the private interests of a member are concerned in a bill or question, he is to withdraw."

And yet the rigid application of this rule would not always be either wise or in the public interest. The argument is often made that a Congressman can and should vote on bills which affect the well-being of his constituents, even if he himself is included. A Congressman who serves a farming district and is himself a farmer, if prohibited from voting on all farm legislation, would not be a very good representative for his district.

Personally I lean toward the view of Plato and Thomas Jefferson, that the best and most practical way to avoid conflict of interest between public and private business is to proscribe private interests for those elected officials whose charge is to serve the public. No Member of Congress, in my judgment, should be permitted to practice law or any other form of private business in which salaries or fees are paid. I feel that Congressional salaries are high enough, and that a Congressman should have no earned income outside his salary.

Over the past decade I have pushed for enactment of legislation covering conflict-of-interest cases. When he was elected President, John F. Kennedy appointed a special panel to study conflict-of-interest problems in government, and the New York City Bar Association undertook a study of its own. A new Federal conflict-of-interest law was finally signed in January, 1963. It strengthened Title 18 of the United States Code, pertaining to bribery, graft, and conflict of interest among government employees, including Members of Congress, and prohibited payment to Members of Congress for services rendered before Federal agencies in matters of "direct and substantial interest" to the government. The act also restricted, but did not prohibit, the practice of law by current Members of Congress. A heavy penalty was written into the act.

At present there is a double standard for Congress and the executive branch in conflict-of-interest cases. The law requires that Federal officials disclose and divest themselves of outside interests, but the standard Congress applies to its own Members is far weaker than the one it applies to the executive branch. Presidential orders in 1961 and again in 1966 spelled out guidelines for employees of the Federal executive branch. The Congress has been quick to harp on the dangers of conflict of interest in the executive branch, but it never seems to apply the sermon to its own Members.

Congressmen are often asked to make representations to Federal agencies, especially regulatory agencies, on behalf of constituents. Many of these ex-parte communications potentially involve conflicts of interest, and in my view these requests should always be in writing and open to public scrutiny.

Two other ethical problems merit consideration. First, nepotism. The appointment of relatives to government positions on a public payroll is a problem that goes back at least as far as government itself. A news story in 1967 reported that one tenth of all Members of the House of Representatives had relatives on their office payrolls. The fact that a few have abused this privilege has reflected badly on many dedicated and hard-working employees of the Congress. A wide-ranging Federal law was passed in 1967, prohibiting the appointment of any relative to a position on a public payroll by any Federal official, including the President and Members of Congress.

The other problem is the expenditure of public funds on foreign travel—in the vernacular, junketing. A 1968 survey showed 41 percent of all Members of Congress used Federal government funds on reported trips outside the United States. Because of our nation's widespread interests throughout the world, a certain amount of foreign travel is desirable for on-the-spot inspections of both defense and nondefense establishments. But there have also been notorious examples of waste and extravagance at the expense of the public. All public funds spent on foreign travel should be closely checked to assure that tax monies are properly spent.

Significant progress has been made in the field of government ethics over the last two decades. My first years in Congress, beginning in 1949, saw a rash of Congressional investigations into such groups as the five percenters, organized crime, and the Reconstruction Finance Company. Several of these inquiries led to large-scale public scandals.

In 1951 a small group of Congressmen began meeting informally to talk about what could be done to check these flagrant breaches of public ethics. I was asked to chair the group, which soon focused its attention on drafting a code of ethics for government service. For seven years we worked first on the language and then to enlist the support of the Congressional leadership.

The Code of Ethics for Government Service was finally approved by the Congress in 1958. Its passage was a milestone in Congressional and governmental ethics, although in its final form the legislation did not include all the teeth needed for full enforcement. The ten points of the code cover all Federal employees, including Members of Congress:

Any person in Government service should:

1. Put loyalty to the highest moral principles and to country above loyalty to persons, party, or Government department.

2. Uphold the Constitution, laws, and legal regulations of the United States and of all governments therein and never be a party to their evasion.

3. Give a full day's labor for a full day's pay; giving to the performance of his duties his earnest effort and best thought.

4. Seek to find and employ more efficient and economical ways of getting tasks accomplished.

5. Never discriminate unfairly by the dispensing of special favors or privileges to anyone, whether for remuneration or not; and never accept, for himself or his family, favors or benefits under circumstances which might be construed by reasonable persons as influencing the performance of his governmental duties.

6. Make no private promises of any kind binding upon the duties of office, since a government employee has no private word which can be binding on public duty.

7. Engage in no business with the Government, either directly or indirectly, which is inconsistent with the conscientious performance of his governmental duties.

8. Never use any information coming to him confidentially in the performance of governmental duties as a means for making private profit.

9. Expose corruption wherever discovered.

10. Uphold these principles, ever conscious that public office is a public trust.

The 1958 Code of Ethics became a model for several state and local government codes. A former chairman of the Civil Service Commission wrote: "Passage by the Congress of . . . a uniform code of ethics in the federal service was a major contribution in this field. It has done much to stimulate awareness of responsibility for employee conduct, and to emphasize to employees the importance of their duties."

Public ethics is one of those fields where major progress seems to follow hard on the heels of scandal. The next important step in Congressional ethics came in 1963, following a public furore over the activities of Bobby Baker, a former page boy who became secretary of the Senate. Baker was charged with using his government position improperly to further his private interests.

At the start of the investigation I wrote to Senator B. Everett Jordan of North Carolina, chairman of the Rules Committee, making several suggestions as to how the Senate might strengthen its rules to prevent similar conflict-of-interest cases in the future. One of these proposals was that the Senate should establish a bipartisan grievance committee, patterned after the Bar Association's grievance group, which would be empowered to investigate Senators and their employees and recommend disciplinary action to the Senate. This committee could also require full disclosure of Senators' personal income and investments.

I had already introduced this idea in the House, and when hearings on the case began in the Senate, I testified, urging the Rules Committee to report out a resolution calling for a Senate ethics committee. Senator John Sherman Cooper of Kentucky, a member of the Rules Committee, took up the idea and introduced a bill to establish the first ethics committee in the Congress. The Rules Committee turned down Senator Cooper's resolution, six to three, but on July 24, 1964, the Senate took up a Rules Committee proposal to broaden its own jurisdiction to allow it to investigate violation of Senate rules by a Member and recommend appropriate disciplinary action to the Senate. Senator Cooper then offered his resolution again as an amendment to the bill reported out by the Rules Committee—and by a vote of fifty to thirty-three, the Senate agreed to create the Select Committee on Standards of Conduct. The committee has since served a useful purpose, once bringing the improprieties of a Senator to the attention of the country, and generally having a salutory effect on Senatorial conduct.

It was the flagrant case of Adam Clayton Powell, Jr., that finally sparked similar action in the House of Representatives. In the summer of 1966 committee members of his own party took the unusual step of drawing public attention to the activities of the New York Congressman, chairman of the House Education and Labor Committee. Representative Powell had earlier been cited by a New York Supreme Court Justice for his failure to pay a woman who had won a defamation-of-character suit against him three years before. In Congress he was widely criticized for having on his office payroll his wife, who lived in Puerto Rico but did not work for the government, and for misusing committee funds, particularly airline credit cards.

For many years I had been pushing for an ethics committee in the House, similar to the one created in the Senate in 1964. Public demand that Congress do something about the conduct of the Member from Harlem led the House of Representatives to adopt my resolution, establishing an ethics committee after the model of the Bar Association's Grievance Committee. On October 19, 1966, by a vote of 265 to zero, the House approved its first ethics committee, the Select Committee on Standards of Conduct. I was named chairman by the Speaker of the House, John W. McCormack of Massachusetts.

The committee was a watered-down version of my original proposal, and it functioned only for a short period of time. But it did recommend the establishment of a permanent ethics committee in the House, and in 1967 the House adopted the report and its recommendations.

Shortly thereafter the House approved its own Code of Ethics, drafted by the new permanent committee. (See Appendix II.) At the same time it strengthened the disclosure law for Members of the House and principal staff members. The new disclosure law was a big improvement, but I still believe that full disclosure should be required, and I have introduced a bill to that effect.

The 1960's in the United States have been years of sweeping reform in the field of government ethics. Prodded by the public to check flagrant abuse of public trust, the Congress enacted a Code of Ethics for Government Service, established ethics committees in the House and Senate, and required all Federal employees, including Members of Congress, to disclose assets and outside income. Outside the Federal government, state and local governments have put new and stronger ethics laws on their own books.

Much has been accomplished. Outright instances of immoral practice in government are substantially fewer today than in previous decades of American history. Yet much remains to be done. We still need more than the Ten Commandments and the Sermon on the Mount to deter men from unethical behavior. Ethics committees should be equipped with strong disciplinary powers as well as the standards of conduct set forth in the codes; as Thomas Hobbes pointed out, "Covenants without the sword are but empty words." If our deistic tradition of the goodness of man were sufficient to explain man's moral behavior, then we would need nothing more than codes to ensure honesty and decency in government. But history has taught us, at times painfully, that people often act more in accordance with the Calvinist doctrine of man's original depravity, and for that reason we continue to need preventive sanctions even in the highest councils of government.

In the best-governed societies, some mistakes are made. Our own Constitution provides checks against some of the worst of these mistakes. For example, when a bad law is enacted by Congress, the courts may challenge its constitutionality by the process of judicial review. Similarly, most elected officials have short terms and must submit themselves for public review in order to be reelected.

Still, the average citizen often feels he has no recourse against unfair decisions or improper treatment by public officials. He may go to his Congressman or Senator for assistance, but they have other heavy responsibilities and often cannot take the time required to see that complaints are carefully reviewed. Some have suggested the appointment of ombudsmen to investigate citizens' complaints, after the model of Sweden and New Zealand. An ombudsman is a government official appointed to receive and investigate complaints of abuses or capricious acts by public officials.

My own preference would be for a court of ethics which would render decisions on alleged improprieties in government—legislative, executive, and judicial. Theoretically, cases of serious misbehavior are supposed to be handled by impeachment. But as a practical matter only questions of very grave consequence are so handled; and in fact impeachment has traditionally been limited to cases of outright moral turpitude. The American people deserve better oversight of the deportment of government officials. In my opinion the Fortas affair, in which a Supreme Court Justice resigned under fire for the first time in the Court's history, is the sort of case that could be handled by a court of ethics.

For several years I have introduced legislation to establish such a court of ethics. As outlined in my bill, the court would hear complaints of unethical conduct, and if the charges proved factual, it would hold hearings and render decisions. It could also make advisory decisions in advance of any questionable behavior when asked to do so. Complaints would have to be based on established law or resolution, including the statutes in Title 18 of the U.S. Code, the criminal statutes, and the Code of Ethics for Government Service.

Winston Churchill once said that democracy is the worst form of government except for all the other systems that have been tried. It is certainly the most difficult. It requires more of us—character, self-restraint, a willingness to serve the public interest as well as our private interests. In contrast to Catherine de Medici's France, government in the United States is responsible to the people; that is the basic reason why high standards of conduct must be required of our officials.

Because we offer more opportunity and more freedom to the individual in this country, we require more responsibility and moral fiber from our citizens. I feel this lesson in responsibility and commitment to an honest life should begin at an early age, and for that reason I would favor the teaching of high ethical standards in schools, to educate our children in morals as well as mind.

We are fortunate that a sound governmental process has been established in America, and that over the years we have made progress, albeit slow, in public morality. Yet our political leaders will continue to face pressures of all kinds, and unless they continue to show faith in their religion and faith in our system, we will not survive as a nation. Man's problems today are not so much with the new atom as with the old Adam.

Improving the hearts and souls of individual men is still the greatest objective of mankind, and each one of us can do our part by improving ourselves so that we may meet the challenges of our day and point the way to greater days for our children and their children.

CHURCH
AND STATE
IN AMERICA

☆ ☆

by Congressman
ALBERT H. QUIE

ALBERT H. QUIE

Congressman Albert H. Quie, now in his sixth term as Republican Representative from Dennison, Minnesota, has been called the GOP's Mr. Education. As the second-ranking Republican on the House Education and Labor Committee, he is acknowledged as one of the leading Congressional experts on education and has played a major role in shaping important recent education legislation. In 1968 he received the National Education Association's Distinguished Service Award.

A committed Christian, Congressman Quie has said, "Everybody must share his faith. We do whether we realize it or not. People expect good things from you as a Christian, and if they don't see good things, then your witness is negative." He has written articles for religious periodicals, and is coauthor of an essay in *Republican Papers,* entitled "Poverty in America."

Church and State in America

Almighty God, we acknowledge our dependence upon Thee, and we beg Thy blessings upon us, our parents, our teachers and our country.

In 1962 this simple prayer touched off one of the most bitter controversies in American legal history. The New York State Board of Regents had published the prayer in their Statement on Moral and Spiritual Training in the Schools, and approved its use in school-opening ceremonies. But the parents of ten New York schoolchildren felt that their rights were being infringed and brought suit against the Regents, challenging the constitutionality of state and local laws which authorized recitation of the prayer in New York schools.

In *Engel v. Vitale* the Supreme Court of the United States ruled that the laws authorizing the prayer were in violation of the First Amendment. In the majority opinion, Justice Black wrote:

We agree with the contention since we think that the constitutional prohibition against laws respecting an establishment of religion must at least mean that in this country it is no part of the business of government to compose official prayers for any group of the American people to recite as part of a religious program carried on by government.

Reading of the Scriptures as part of the opening exercises of public school was declared unconstitutional by the Court in *Abington School District v. Schempp*. In a parallel case brought against the Baltimore School Commissioners, the High Court agreed with a trial court's finding that Bible reading was a religious ceremony and was intended to be so by the state. Consequently the Court ruled that "the exercises and the law requiring them are in violation of the Establishment Clause." In concluding the majority opinion, Justice Clark wrote: "In the relationship between man and religion, the State is firmly committed to a position of neutrality."

The effect of these two opinions was to reopen a question as old as the Republic and to set off a heated public discussion of that delicate, time-honored issue, the relationship between church and state. There was compliance in New York, defiance in Alabama, and a furore in the halls of Congress. Christians differed widely in their reactions to the decisions. Some favored the outcome while many sought to modify or reverse it through proposed amendments to the Constitution.

In the Eighty-eighth Congress (1963–64), no fewer than 156 Senate and House Joint Resolutions were introduced to amend the Constitution to allow prayer and Bible reading in the schools. One popular, broad-brush resolution would have permitted "offering, reading from, or listening to prayers or biblical Scriptures, if participation therein is on a voluntary basis, in any governmental or public school, institution or place." It also would have permitted reference to God or a Supreme Being in almost every governmental activity. Another proposed amendment merely sought to authorize "non-denominational religious observances through the invocation of the blessing of God or the recitation of prayer . . . if participation therein is not made compulsory."

After extensive hearings in the spring of 1964, the House Judiciary Committee decided against taking further action to bring the issue before the House of Representatives. During these hearings many religious leaders opposed a constitutional amendment. They were worried about the possible effects of an amendment which might some day allow preference to one particular branch of organized religion.

But the issue was not dead. The Eighty-ninth Congress saw the introduction of fifty-six joint resolutions, with wide variation in language. In an effort to narrow objection to the issues raised in *Engel v. Vitale,* one Senate resolution simply called for an amendment permitting voluntary participation in school prayers, and specified that no authority could prescribe the form or content of any prayer. Even this language failed to obtain the necessary two-thirds majority when it was offered as an amendment to another resolution under debate in the Senate.

A further revision offered in the Ninetieth Congress proposed an amendment stating that nothing in the Constitution should abridge the right of persons lawfully assembled in any public building to participate in nondenominational prayer. No action was taken on it by the Congress.

The Supreme Court decisions on prayer and Bible reading in the schools were landmark cases in the modern history of church-state relations. But there has been a marked and significant change in the issues since the adoption of the First Amendment, and it would be well to look for a moment at how this controversy first entered American history.

Congress shall make no law respecting an establishment of religion, or prohibiting the free exercise thereof; . . .

With these few words, the Bill of Rights proscribes the Congress from establishing a state church or from interfering with the exercise of any citizen's religion. The Founding Fathers felt so strongly about the issue that they made it the First Amendment. They had already taken care, in Article Six of the Constitution, to prohibit any religious test for candidates for public office. The language of both sections appeared quite straightforward. Yet, the controversy over *Engel v. Vitale* is but the latest in a long history of arguments about the meaning of the First Amendment and the proper relationship between church and state in America.

A brief look at the origins of the amendment may help us to understand the problem. Its language had been revised at each step of the legislative process in its course through the House of Representatives, the Senate, and the conference committee. The proposal as originally phrased read: "The civil rights of none shall be abridged on account of religious belief or worship, nor shall any national religion be established, nor shall the full and equal rights of conscience be in any manner, or on any pretense, infringed." This phraseology suggests how highly the framers of the amendment valued the individual's right to follow any religion he desired. The prohibition against establishing a state church was considered an integral part of this protection of individual rights.

Why was this necessary? From experience in their homelands, where state churches had been established, the framers of the amendment recognized the stultifying effect state support for religion had on the fervor of its adherents. State support meant taxation of nonbelievers, agnostics, and members of other fellowships to finance the operation of the state church—obviously an interference with individual rights of conscience. Taxation for religious purposes also deprived the individual of a vital aspect of his Christianity: returning to God a tithe of his material substance. Private and religious philanthropy lost its significance under these circumstances.

Perhaps most important, many of the early American colonists had had firsthand experience of religious persecution at the hands of an established church. The Church of England had done little to discourage the persecution of "papists," Dissenters, and others who strayed from the official creed. Puritan Separatists in Massachusetts, Catholics in Maryland, Quakers in Pennsylvania—each had felt the oppression of a state church in the Old World.

Yet the irony is that, when they arrived in the New World, many of these early settlers turned around and established state churches of their own. In varying degrees the writers and ratifiers of each state charter believed that the state should be committed to one denomination and that others should be discouraged. A majority in each state felt the establishment of one church was essential to its growth.

The establishment of these churches took several forms and reached into many aspects of life in the different states. In Virginia, the salaries of clergymen were fixed by law; dissenters paid taxes for the support of the Anglican church, and the children of parents married outside the Anglican communion were legally illegitimate. In the Carolinas and Georgia dissenters and Catholics were disfranchised at various times. In Connecticut full citizenship had been denied to non-Congregationalists from the beginning of the New Haven colony in 1639; the legislature was required to confirm the election of a new minister by a church, and legislative sanction was required to establish a new church.

Some states denied voting rights to persons outside the state church, or prohibited members of nonestablished churches from holding public office. In Puritan Massachusetts, full citizenship was limited to those who enjoyed a "covenant relationship" with God, as determined by the elders of the local congregation. Fines were often imposed for nonattendance at church. Massachusetts was a theocracy, a state ruled by God, and the clergy were expected to guide in fashioning the laws. Purity of doctrine was zealously guarded; a 1646 Act Against Heresy provided for the expulsion of anyone who questioned certain doctrines like the immortality of the soul. Anne Hutchinson was driven out of the colony for the heresy of Antinomianism; Roger Williams was forced to flee because he believed church and state should be separate. A number of Quakers were executed when they defied decrees of expulsion. At the end of the seventeenth century the notorious Salem witchcraft trials provided further evidence of the dangers of mixing civil and spiritual authority.

By the time of the American Revolution many colonial leaders felt that in the interests of religious freedom the power of the state churches had to be curbed. The Great Awakening and other evangelistic movements had brought Presbyterians, Baptists and Methodists into the mainstream of American religious life, and these groups now insisted that their rights of conscience be protected. When the Virginia State Convention met in 1776 to consider a Virginia Bill of Rights, a popular tide was running in support of disestablishing the Anglican state church. Patrick Henry, in the first draft of an article on religious freedom, offered the proviso:

That Religion, or the duty that we owe to our Creator, and the manner of discharging it, can be directed only by reason and conviction, and not by force or violence; and therefore that all men should enjoy the fullest toleration of the exercise of religion according to the dictates of conscience, unpunished and unrestrained by the magistrate, unless under color of religion that any man disturbed the peace, the happiness, or safety of society; and that it is the mutual duty of all to practice Christian forbearance, love and charity towards each other.

By 1785, Virginia was ready to go the whole distance. The Declaratory Act, generally credited to the inspiration of Thomas Jefferson, provided:

Be it enacted by the General Assembly, that no man shall be compelled to frequent or support any religious worship, place or ministry whatever; nor shall be enforced, restrained, molested or burthened in his body of goods, nor shall otherwise suffer on account of his religious opinions or belief; but that all men shall be free to profess, and by argument to maintain, their opinion in matters of religion, and the same shall in no wise diminish, enlarge or affect their civil capacities.

Jefferson's thinking deeply influenced the authors of the First Amendment. Though he was in France at the time the Bill of Rights was drawn up, his friend James Madison was a key figure in formulating the language of this and other amendments. There was general agreement on the need to protect all citizens from any infringement of rights by the Federal government through the establishment of a Federal church. The Constitution, by omission of references to God in its text, and by prohibiting religious tests for officeholders, implied that there would be no state church. However, the framers of the Bill of Rights desired specific language on this score.

When presented to the House by Madison, the wording was revised to read: "No religion shall be established by law, nor shall the equal rights of conscience be infringed." Records of House debate show objection to the wording by one Representative who believed that the amendment was unnecessary since the states had not, in the Constitution, given the Federal government the right to establish a church. Another Representative thought guarantee of the rights of conscience should be written into the amendment as well as protection of the right to follow no religion.

Madison suggested addition of the word "national" before religion since he thought the people feared the possibility of one denomination's ascendancy, but the proposal was defeated by Representatives who objected to the thought that the new Federal government would be viewed as a national government.

As passed by the House the amendment read: "Congress shall make no law establishing religion, or to prevent the free exercise thereof, or to infringe the rights of conscience." The Senate preferred a simpler version: "Congress shall make no law establishing articles of religion." The final language, worked out by a joint committee of Senators and Representatives, restored the House provision against laws preventing the free exercise of religion, but used more ambiguous wording "respecting an establishment" of religion.

It is worth noting again that, despite widespread opposition to a *federally* established church, almost all the state constitutions referred to God in their texts and provided for an established *state* religion. The people were essentially religious, but feared to give the Federal government the power to establish a "national" religion.

From this it would appear that political considerations rather than religious beliefs were most important in reaching final agreement on the First Amendment. The amendment protected the union from the divisive effects that the establishment of a national church would have had on states supporting other denominations. At the same time, it protected the individual's right to practice his own religion without persecution by the Federal government.

So religious freedom was written into the Constitution and ratified by the several states. Yet there was by no means universal agreement on Thomas Jefferson's doctrine of a "wall of separation" between church and state. Several states continued religious tests for public office well into the nineteenth century. The church-state issue had not been settled. Let us look now at some of the forms it has taken in our own day.

★ ★ ★

Contemporary issues involving the relationship between church and state have included questions of the taxation of churches, social-security benefits for ministers, the administration of government education programs by religious bodies, public aid to hospitals operated under religious auspices, the Food for Peace program, and, most significantly, a number of issues in which the organized church has been brought into potential conflict with the state in the field of education. In almost all of these questions, purists have insisted that the First Amendment requires absolute separation between church and state; they believe there should be no communication between the two.

It is my view that the First Amendment does not seek to establish a wall of separation so that no communication is possible between church and state. To restrict such communication to the extent the purists desire would make it impossible for state legislatures and the Congress to consider knowledgeably any change in the laws affecting churches. Who would present to the legislative bodies the views of the church and the effect of proposed changes on organized religion?

The question of taxing churches and the history of the coverage of Christian ministers under social security provides a good illustration of the problems posed by such a rigid interpretation. In carrying out the intent of the First Amendment, the Congress and local governments have refrained from taxing churches and their charitable instrumentalities. But when social security was introduced, and as more and more occupations were included in social-security coverage, the question arose as to whether ministers should become eligible for its benefits. In the early years, there was unquestionably conscientious objection to the idea of offering any form of state security to ministers. Later, when hearings before the House Ways and Means Committee had shown that some ministers did desire coverage, the problem arose as to whether the government had the right to tax a church, as the minister's employer.

Interpreting the First Amendment to prohibit taxation of churches, the committee wisely offered ministers the option of obtaining voluntary coverage through the provisions covering self-employed individuals. Under this portion of the law, the self-employed person pays a larger tax to compensate for the lack of the employer's matching contribution. The church-state issue was sidestepped by making participation voluntary on the part of the clergyman.

Under the administrative procedures, a clergyman could elect coverage within a specified time period. This appeared to raise no Constitutional problem. Actually, over the years, several clergymen, who approached retirement age, desired to change their original election. Consequently, the committee and the Congress amended the law on several occasions to extend the period within which the election could be made. Finally, in the 1967 social security amendments, the committee recommended that clergymen be mandatorily covered, but with an escape clause for persons who conscientiously objected to the social-security system. It is important that the churches as organizations express their views on the effect of legislation on their institutions and their officials.

The church-state issue came up again during hearings on the war-on-poverty bill in 1964. Under the Community Action program, Community Action Councils were authorized to fund remedial-education programs aimed at removing obstacles to learning among preschool children from low-income families. Administration witnesses testified that some of these projects—now called Head Start— could be administered by church groups. As the program has been implemented, it is not uncommon for churches to administer Head Start projects.

To help students from low-income families attend college, work training and college work-study programs were established. However, provisions were inserted in the legislation so that no payment could be made for work involving the construction, operation or maintenance of any facility used for sectarian instruction or worship.

Another significant decision in this area was taken when the Congress approved the Hill-Burton Act, providing Federal funds to cover a portion of the cost of constructing new hospitals. Recipient agencies were not restricted to states, counties or municipalities, but included hospitals owned and operated by religious organizations. In this law the Congress recognized the services performed for citizens by church-related hospitals and granted the funds on the basis of those services. Since the beginning of the program an estimated 1,700 church-affiliated hospitals have been granted funds totaling some $722 million.

There are some areas of potential cooperation as well as conflict between church and state. Perhaps no program better illustrates the possibility of parallel interests than what is now called Food for Peace. Originally enacted in the Agricultural Trade Development and Assistance Act of 1954, the program offers surplus agricultural commodities to foreign countries for sale in their own "soft" currencies, or donates these surplus foods to church-related voluntary organizations for free distribution abroad. As the program has developed, the government supplies the charitable agencies with commodities free of charge, pays processing costs if the foods are enriched, packaging costs, ocean freight to the foreign country and internal shipping charges to the distribution point where the voluntary agency has its facilities. In this instance, church organizations provide the mechanism for implementing one of the government's policy goals.

These and other public issues have refocused attention on the relationship between church and state in our own day. But even a brief study of modern church-state controversies establishes the striking fact that the most serious and prolonged debates have dealt not with persecution on religious grounds or taxation of churches but with the education of the nation's children. The Supreme Court decisions on prayer and Bible reading in the schools are good examples of this trend, but there are other major issues in this field—notably the question of public aid to church schools. Let us look now at a few of these issues, and examine some of their potential implications for our society.

Church-state tension in the field of education goes back to the middle of the nineteenth century in America. In 1862 Congress passed the first Morrill Act, which granted each state 30,000 acres times the number of Senators and Representatives from that state, to be used for the support of higher education. Two of the original land-grant colleges —Yale and the University of Delaware—were church-related. Both later dropped their church affiliations around the turn of the century.

The Morrill Act brought the question of state aid to religious schools into the realm of public debate. But it was the Blaine Amendment of 1875 that defined the issue and opened the controversy in earnest. James G. Blaine, a Maine Congressman, offered an amendment to the Constitution before the House of Representatives which would have prevented any state from aiding, directly or indirectly, any church-related school with land or money. The proposal failed to win the necessary two-thirds majority in the Senate, and thus was never brought before the states for ratification. However, its influence is indicated by the fact that between 1877 and 1930, more than thirty states amended their constitutions to prohibit state aid to parochial schools, in addition to the eight states that already had clauses to this effect in their constitutions.

Opponents of the Blaine amendment argued that certain public benefits should be made available to all American schoolchildren, whether in public or private schools. Half a century later, in 1930, the Supreme Court upheld a Louisiana state law which permitted public funds to be spent for textbooks to be lent to students enrolled in public *and* private schools. The petitioners had actually brought suit under the Fourteenth Amendment, claiming that the State Board of Education was taking private property for private uses. The Supreme Court decided in favor of the State Board, arguing that (a) the books were for the use of children, (b) the parochial schools received no actual funds, and (c) the books were nonsectarian. Justice Hughes, in the majority opinion, offered a concise statement of what has come to be called the child-benefit theory:

The schools . . . are not the beneficiaries of these appropriations. They obtain nothing from them, nor are they relieved of a single obligation because of them. The school children and the state alone are the beneficiaries. The legislation does not segregate private schools or their pupils, and its beneficiaries, or attempt to interfere with any matters of exclusively private concern. Its interest is education, broadly; its method comprehensive.

In 1947 the Court extended the principle of public benefits to children in private schools, on the basis of a distinction between profit-making and nonprofit-making private schools. At issue were two statutes: a New Jersey law authorizing school districts to contract for the transportation of students to and from all schools except private schools operated for profit, and a local school-board resolution permitting parents to be reimbursed for sending children to public and nonprofit private schools on public buses. The Court held that this was not a violation of the First Amendment, justifying its decision on grounds that the legislation improved the general welfare of the community. Safe transportation of students was put in the same category as the police and fire protection offered to all religious institutions as a matter of course.

Since the late 1940's there have been a spate of bills dealing directly or indirectly with the question of state aid to church-affiliated schools. One of the most far-reaching and effective education programs enacted by Congress was the so-called G.I. Bill for veterans of World War II. The act provided tuition and fee payments to colleges and monthly support payments to veterans enrolled in accredited institutions for a specified time, depending on the veteran's length of service and the number of his dependents. The program was administered through the schools and no questions were asked about religious affiliation as long as the institution was accredited.

The National School Lunch Act, approved June 4, 1946, provided commodities and cash payments to states to be distributed to local school districts to help pay the cost of nutritious lunches for children. It contained a significant bypass provision which operated in those states where the state constitution prohibited the distribution of funds to parochial and private schools. In such states, the Department of Agriculture could deal directly with the parochial schools. (At the present time, some twenty-six state constitutions prohibit the distribution of funds to parochial schools.) The bypass provision was justified on the basis that the children, not the church, would benefit from the lunches.

Public Law 874 of the Eighty-first Congress, approved on September 30, 1950, provided funds to local school districts which were Federally "impacted"—that is, where Federal installations removed real property from the tax rolls. Under its provisions, the Federal government would contribute to the school district an amount equal to the revenue which would normally be raised from such property. None of the funds were to be allocated to nonpublic schools in the school districts affected.

The National Defense Education Act of 1958 provided benefits only for public schools at the elementary and secondary level but did not discriminate against private schools at the college level. Grants were made to public elementary and secondary schools to purchase laboratory equipment, but only loans were made available to private schools for such purchases.

The Housing Act of 1950 authorized direct loans to institutions of higher education for the construction of housing facilities for students and faculty on interest terms more favorable than those available on the private money market. These loans were made available to church-related colleges and universities. The Housing and Urban Development Act of 1968 and the Higher Education Act Amendments of 1968 both had new provisions to subsidize the interest paid on college-housing mortgages and academic-facility mortgages obtained in the private money market. The subsidy amounted to the difference between the interest rate on the money market and the interest rate charged under the direct-loan program. By this time, no question was raised on the church-state issue.

In 1963 the Higher Education Facilities Act was approved. The act declared that the Federal interest in higher education was so great that grants and loans would be made directly available to institutions of higher education for the construction of academic facilities. Buildings which would be used for sectarian instruction or worship were specifically excluded, but there were no restrictions against grants or loans to church-related colleges and universities for the construction of academic facilities. The grants were constitutionally justified by the child-benefit theory, following the view that it is the student rather than the institution which benefits from the grant.

General acceptance of the child-benefit theory finally made possible the provision of Federal assistance to non-public-school children and teachers. The historic Elementary and Secondary Education Act (ESEA) was signed in 1965. Aimed primarily at meeting the needs of educationally deprived students, it also provided for library materials, audiovisual and laboratory equipment, and other educational services for both public- and nonpublic-school children.

Statistics on educational achievement had dramatically shown that areas of extremely low income and consequent low expenditure for support of education produced large percentages of dropouts, underachievers, and children poorly qualified for life in a highly technological society.

The Federal government had earlier acknowledged its

interest in helping public-school districts whose enrollments were increased by children from nearby Federal installations. By an extension of this logic the Congress now approved legislation providing various kinds of educational materials and services to help school districts upgrade their own programs and especially for disadvantaged children. In ESEA the parochial-school child benefited differently from the way he had benefited in previous cases. The money was to be used for nonpublic-school children but the programs were to be administered by and the materials owned by the public school.

Under Title I of the act, funds were to be distributed to states according to the total number of children from families with incomes below $2,000 and families receiving more than $2,000 in Aid to Families with Dependent Children. The intent was to introduce programs which would help overcome the disadvantages under which educationally deprived children (not just poor children) worked at school. It was hoped that the schools would develop new programs to enrich their curricula and find new means of stimulating the disadvantaged child to high interest and achievement. Schools were given wide leeway to develop what seemed to them to be the most effective programs, even to the extent of providing breakfasts and lunches (supplementing the school lunch program) if it appeared that the children were not learning because of inadequate diets or outright hunger. The local schools were required to organize these programs in such a way that educationally deprived students from nonpublic schools would have the opportunity to participate.

The act also provided funds for the purchase of textbooks and library resources for all children. Students and teachers in nonpublic schools were made eligible to receive books and other resources on a loan basis from the public school. If state constitutions or statutes prevented this, a bypass, similar to that used in the school lunch program, permitted the Federal government to make these materials available through a public agency not affected by such state legal requirements. Another section provided funds for supplementary educational centers and innovative programs; these benefits also were to be made available to nonpublic-school children. Several provisions presented initial administrative difficulties, but these have been largely overcome and nonpublic- as well as public-school children are now receiving considerable benefit from the law.

This 1965 Elementary and Secondary Education Act provided an opportunity to study carefully the implications of church-state cooperation in the field of education. Four years earlier, in 1961, the National Council of Churches had opposed Federal, state and local government grants to nonpublic elementary and secondary schools. At the same time, it supported the provision of dental and medical services, lunches, and other welfare services to all schoolchildren, whether in public or church-related schools, so long as these services could be clearly identified as public services paid for and administered by public authorities.

In implementing such a program, the council recommended several guidelines to avoid any conflict between church and state: (1) Tax revenues should not be given directly to nonpublic elementary and secondary schools. (2) Public officials responsible to the electorate should determine and administer the benefits. (3) Such benefits should be identifiable by students as public services. (4) The inculcation of religion or the teaching of sectarian religion should not be supported. (5) Discrimination in the distribution of benefits by race, religion, or class should not be permitted.

The Christian basis for the council's position was set forth as follows:

Sharing these concerns with a wide range of our fellow citizens, the members of the churches which comprise the National Council of Churches have, in addition, convictions which rise more directly out of their faith in Jesus Christ. That the Kingdom of Christ transcends all nations, that no government of men is independent of God, that the survival of our society depends ultimately upon the providence of God, that no man should be prevented from responding in faith and obedience to God as he is revealed in Jesus Christ: these are some of the specifically Christian convictions that bear upon our attitude toward questions of educational policy in the United States.

A policy statement entitled "The Churches and the Public Schools," adopted by the council's general board in 1963, said:

As Christians we believe that every individual has a right to an education aimed at full development of his capacities as a human being created by God, his character as well as his intellect. We are impelled by the love of neighbor to seek maximum educational opportunities for each individual in order that he may prepare himself for responsible participation in the common life.

Such thinking appeared to be in keeping with the intent of the Elementary and Secondary Education Act—to redress inequalities of opportunity to learn in low-income school districts, whether in public or parochial schools—and representatives of the National Council of Churches supported passage of the bill in testimony before the House Committee on Education and Labor in 1965.

Many people believe that this act stretched the interpretation of the First Amendment to its constitutional limits. But the public interest requires a good educational system, and it is my belief that expansion of Federal financial assistance should be accomplished in such a way that nonpublic-school children will also benefit from Federal programs.

At the same time, the Constitution guarantees each individual the opportunity to worship God as his conscience dictates. This includes the freedom to establish separate school systems to provide for classes of religious instruction. The 1965 Elementary and Secondary Education Act appears to meet the educational interests of the country in both public and nonpublic schools by means of a vehicle which preserves separation of church and state.

★ ★ ★

As we have seen, the relationship between church and state in America has changed dramatically in the 180 years since the beginning of the Republic. The Founding Fathers' primary concern seemed to be to protect citizens against possible religious *oppression* by an established state church. The danger in the eighteenth century seemed to be that some might be persecuted for refusing to adhere to one particular established religion. A number of our early political leaders took it for granted that the state should use its powers to protect and strengthen the church, and that conversely the church should exert a guiding influence over affairs of state. Many believed the ideal form of government was "the rule of God" administered by his servants on earth.

So much has our society changed that few people now fear the tyranny of any church. Today some believe the churches have no business trying to influence public policy in any way. In fact some citizens are beginning to wonder if the freedom to express religious sentiments in public ceremonies may soon come into question. (In some instances schoolchildren have not been permitted to sing Christmas carols.) We are now concerned whether any reference to religion will be *permissible* in public functions. We may be in danger of going from "the rule of God" to "rule without God." Abraham Lincoln warned of this possibility in the middle of the nineteenth century, when the country was torn by civil war:

May we not justly fear that the awful calamity . . . which now desolates the land may be but a punishment inflicted upon us for our presumptuous sins? . . . We have grown in number, wealth, and power as no other nation has ever grown. But we have forgotten God. We have forgotten the gracious hand which preserved us in peace and multiplied and enriched and strengthened us, and we have vainly imagined, in the deceitfulness of our hearts, that all these blessings were produced by some superior wisdom and virtue of our own. Intoxicated with unbroken success, we have become too self-sufficient to feel the necessity of redeeming and preserving grace, too proud to pray to the God who made us.

We have noted the shift in church-state controversy to questions of educational policy. I believe this is a highly significant change, for what is finally at issue is the power of any highly organized body—be it the church or the state or some other institution—to influence the teaching of values in our schools and the training of young minds.

Historically we have recognized the responsibility of the state to provide a decent education for all children in our society, at the same time acknowledging that some parents may prefer a religious education for their children, of the sort that it would be improper for the state to provide. Both institutions have wielded great power, often unnoticed and unchecked, in the formation of core values that govern future lives. Today both have at their disposal the increasingly powerful tools of mass communications, social psychology, and staff expertise. The question whether any highly organized institution should be permitted to exercise such power without careful scrutiny by individual parents and citizens may become a primary question for public debate in the 1970's.

This is not to suggest that we no longer have to worry about undue influence of the church over the state, or vice versa, in education or other areas of public policy. But in my opinion the church has more to fear than the state in these situations, whereas in the eighteenth century the danger was the reverse. At the national level, the government is now so huge and overpowering that church policy would have little impact on it. However, where a church receives public funds to administer government programs—as in Project Head Start—the government's policies must be adopted by the church-related institution, as a look at the guidelines laid down for Federal programs will show.

Yet I believe there are three important ways in which religious influence can justifiably be brought to bear on the state. First, a Christian citizen has a right and responsibility, protected by our Constitution and laws, to express his views to the state in all areas of government. As a member of the church, his conscience is developed on moral questions, and the influence of the religious teachings he has received affects his views on public issues. The citizen can accept as much or as little of the church's teachings as he wants, but to this extent they are his own views rather than the views of the organized church. There should be no legal prohibition against his influencing the state by peaceable means.

Secondly, there are moral questions on which church and citizens speak in concert. Traditionally many churches and citizens' groups have joined forces in opposition to gambling, prostitution and other forms of vice, or the sale of alcoholic beverages. But today we see both church and citizens speaking out on such issues as civil rights, feeding the hungry, and the use of national resources to wage war. Speaking in concert, the organized church and citizens have had a dramatic impact on the state, especially in developing public opinion.

The third means through which the church speaks in an acceptable way is through its organization. Whenever the question of taxation of church property comes up in legislative bodies or revenue agencies, the church as an organization is expected to express its views and deal directly with the state in receiving tax exemption. Similarly, when the government purchases services for hospital, welfare and feeding programs administered by churches, it deals directly with the churches in the preparation and operation of these programs. Finally, because of the effect public-education policy has on parochial education, the organized church is directly concerned with the formulation of that policy. Where aid for higher education is received directly, or where public policy on education influences church-related education, the church not only has the opportunity to speak out, but we should expect it to do so.

Church-state relations have changed greatly since the beginning of our history. In all probability they will continue to evolve and change in the years ahead, as the problems which face us evolve and change. The First Amendment has served us well, ensuring freedom of conscience and setting religion outside the proper responsibility of government; I believe most Americans are firmly convinced of its wisdom. At the same time, I hope that our local, state and national governments will continue to be informed by the spirit and concern of the churches, for much of our strength as a nation is drawn directly from our religious heritage. The French observer Alexis de Tocqueville, in his book *Democracy in America,* expressed it simply and poetically:

I sought for the greatness and genius of America in her commodious harbors and her ample rivers, and it was not there; in her fertile fields and boundless prairies, and it was not there. Not until I went into the churches of America, and heard her pulpits aflame with righteousness, did I understand the secret of her genius and power. America is great because she is good, and if America ever ceases to be good, America will cease to be great.

AMERICAN PROTESTANTISM AND POLITICAL IDEOLOGY

by Congressman
JOHN B. ANDERSON

JOHN B. ANDERSON

Congressman John B. Anderson, third-ranking Republican in the House of Representatives, is now serving his fifth term as a Representative from Rockford, Illinois. Elected chairman of the House Republican Conference by his GOP colleagues in January, 1969, he is widely regarded as one of the most articulate and forceful speakers in the House. As second-ranking Republican on the powerful House Rules Committee, he deals with virtually every major piece of legislation that comes to the House floor; in addition he sits on the Joint Atomic Energy Committee.

Congressman Anderson has long been an active lay leader in the Evangelical Free Church. A member and former trustee of the First Evangelical Free Church of Rockford, he has served on the Board of Education of Trinity College in Chicago, and in 1964 was named Outstanding Layman of the Year by the National Association of Evangelicals. He has written chapters of two books—*We Propose: A Modern Congress* and *Republican Papers*—and has contributed articles to such journals as *Theology Today, Contact,* and other religious publications.

American Protestantism and Political Ideology

Politicians make unholy alliances, so the legend goes, and presumably preachers make holy ones. The analogy is not terribly profound, perhaps, but it does have the advantage of clarity and it fits comfortably into conventional canons of casual conversation. However, we run afoul of clarity and profundity all at once when we consider the compacts that preachers sometimes make with politicians. Are such alliances holy or unholy, sacred or suspect?

As both a Member of Congress and an active Protestant layman, I have been intrigued for some time by the tacit alliances between political and religious conservatism on the one hand, and political and religious liberalism on the other. These relationships are unofficial and often indistinct, but it is clear that they do exist and that they have made their own contribution to both our religious and political culture. Are there substantive reasons for these ideological affinities? What are the inherent strengths and weaknesses of such an alignment of interests?

Some students would attribute these alliances—whether holy or not—to the inherent logic in each of two different world views. They contend that a religious liberal, if he follows the premises of his faith to their logical conclusions, is bound to become a political liberal. Similarly a religious conservative ought to be conservative politically if he is faithful to the presuppositions of his religious beliefs.

Other students of this connection between political and religious persuasions insist that it follows not from logical but from psychological laws. They maintain that the link between the isms has little or nothing to do with rational deduction, but rather stems from the basic psychic orientation of individuals. William James, in *The Varieties of Religious Experience,* held that a man's religious experience will be conditioned by his primary personality traits; *e.g.,* if he is hardheaded in his approach to life, he will be less likely to acknowledge dependence on God. Similarly, those who would explain political and religious ties in psychological terms maintain that these ties simply show an inner disposition on the part of the individual toward liberal or conservative persuasions per se, regardless of their contents. Thus a person does not think through his political and religious commitments so much as he acts out his own psychic drives.

In my view, neither of these viewpoints offers a satisfactory explanation of the interrelationships between religious and political conservatism and their liberal counterparts. I take issue with the cynics and behaviorists who would deny man's capacity to deal rationally with social, moral and political issues. At the same time, having seen at firsthand these strange alignments between our religious and political cultures, I am hard put to explain them on a completely rational basis.

If we look at the contemporary situation, for example, we find that the National Council of Churches—an essentially liberal religious body—generally takes what we call, in our somewhat confused political lexicon, a liberal position in its pronouncements on public policy questions. By contrast, the National Association of Evangelicals—an essentially conservative religious council—regularly takes a conservative position on political questions although it is less inclined to public policy statements. And the American Council of Christian Churches, composed mainly of small, independent, Fundamentalist congregations, takes an even more conservative bent on public issues, sometimes aligning itself with the radical right.

Examples are legion. In the area of civil rights, the National Council of Churches has pushed for more vigorous action on the part of Congress, while the National Association of Evangelicals has persistently warned against the attempt to legislate morality. In foreign policy, the first group calls for the recognition of Communist China while the other asks continued support for the Nationalist government on Formosa. The first praises recent Supreme Court decisions governing rights of the accused; the other condemns them. The first endorses Supreme Court rulings which limit public prayer and religious observances in the public schools; the other seeks to reverse these decisions.

I do not wish to equate either of these groups with virtue or evil. I am simply wondering out loud why this relationship exists between conservative religious groups and conservative political interests, and between certain liberal elements of American Protestantism and liberal political groups. Are there dogmatic presuppositions within each religious community which demand these political conclusions? Or are these tacit alliances psychological and irrational? Or does the answer lie elsewhere?

(I should like to make clear at the outset that when I speak of conservatives and liberals, the right and the left, I do not mean to include the lunatic fringes that exist at both ends of the political spectrum. Those on the far left, of course, disclaim any sort of religious philosophy, at least insofar as it embraces the Judeo-Christian ethic. Those on the far right more often than not do profess a religious basis for their political beliefs, but it is not our purpose here to analyze those distortions of basic Christian truths.)

The longer I have looked at them, the more convinced I have become that there are no easy answers to the questions we have posed. A poll conducted by the magazine *Christianity Today* at the beginning of the Ninety-first Congress sheds little light on the matter. All 535 Members of the House and Senate were listed by church membership, and aside from those few who professed membership in no organized church, the poll indicated that some of our most liberal Members from a political standpoint were associated with denominations usually considered extremely conservative from the theological point of view. It occurred to me then that, the central thesis of this essay notwithstanding, you don't necessarily tell a politician by his church pew.

But in seeking to relate my own religious convictions to my political life, I have been forced to make some tentative judgments as to why we so often find conservative political philosophies in league with conservative theologies, while liberal politicians often end up working closely with liberal churchmen. Having offered the warning "Let the reader beware," I should like to share the observations which have made this phenomenon in American political culture comprehensible to me.

Broadly speaking, there are three basic reasons for the alliances between religious and political isms of the right and left: (1) The relationships are partially rooted in the history of American Protestantism, in which the growth of the Social Gospel movement coincided with and developed into a challenge to religious orthodoxy itself. (2) The relationships are in part illusory, due to confusion in our use of the terms "liberal" and "conservative" in American political culture. And (3) the relationships are partly dogmatic and partly psychological, illustrating merely that the political animal is neither so irrational as the behaviorists would have us think, nor so rational as our Enlightenment heritage would lead us to believe.

Let us first put the problem into historical perspective. The American religious heritage was essentially orthodox, Calvinistic and evangelical in character. This is not to deny the deistic persuasion of many of our great eighteenth-century leaders, nor is it to deny the influence of Wesleyan theology or the later infusion of Roman Catholic thinking into our religious culture. But in the early stages of American history, orthodox, Calvinistic, and evangelical religious thought played a major role in establishing the primary motifs of our political culture. Indeed, it is difficult to separate the religious strains from the political in such colonial documents as the Mayflower Compact and Thomas Hooker's Fundamental Orders of Connecticut. In many colonies clergymen actually governed the process of political enfranchisement at their own discretion.*

Early orthodox thinkers affirmed the literal inspiration of the Bible, and saw no reason to doubt such Biblical miracles as the virgin birth of Christ, his visible and bodily return, or the literal establishment of the Kingdom of God beyond earthly society. Indeed, the doctrines of religious orthodoxy were essentially the doctrines we attribute to fundamentalism today. Seen from this perspective, fundamentalism is basically a movement to preserve religious orthodoxy in the face of challenges from religious liberalism in the nineteenth and twentieth centuries.

Orthodox Christian thought heavily influenced the way

* See Albert Quie, "Church and State in America," pp. 133–34.

in which Americans looked at the social order and tried to deal with it. The imprint of the doctrine of the sinfulness of fallen man is clearly seen in the Constitution, which implicitly recognized that neither any man nor any government, nor any branch thereof, could be trusted with unlimited powers. The doctrine of the separation of powers, so fundamental to the evolution of American constitutional government, found its inspiration not only in Rousseau and Montesquieu but in Genesis and the subsequent books of the Old and New Testaments. While European philosophers and social theorists were talking about a new Enlightenment Man who could be educated to become the perfect social being, the writers of the *Federalist Papers* were stressing the fact that man would always be susceptible to his own self-interests and passions. Thus, representation in the Congress was to be indirect; there were to be checks and balances within the government; and all government power was to be limited by the Constitution itself. The election of a President was to be accomplished not by the direct vote of the people but by an Electoral College, composed of men of some educational attainment and social position who could make a wiser choice than the great mass of the untutored population.

Second, orthodox Christians believed strongly in a Kingdom of God separate from human society here on earth. While there were attempts to model society on the Word of God and to make it as responsive as possible to his will, there was general agreement that only God himself could usher in the perfect and everlasting Kingdom. A literal interpretation of the Pauline gospel furnished the doctrinal underpinning; in I Corinthians 15:22–24 (RSV) Saint Paul wrote:

For as in Adam all die, so also in Christ shall all be made alive. But each in his own order: Christ, the first fruits, then at his coming those who belong to Christ. Then comes the end, when he delivers the kingdom to God the Father after destroying every rule and every authority and every power.

Again, we miss the significance of this point unless we remember that European thinkers at this time were arguing for the creation of civil religions which would take the place of the church. Americans, by contrast, were working out a way to separate church and state—not because they felt religious values should not be recognized in government, but because they wanted to preserve the separate functions of each, as well as to protect individual freedom of conscience against encroachment by the state.* Seen in this light, the Constitution was not so much a concession of power to a new government as a statement of the limitations placed upon its power. While the new government had obligations in the public sector, it was not chartered to create a new society. The new society, for the orthodox Christian, was to be ushered in through the church and the return of Christ—not the state. Had not Saint John foretold the coming of a New Jerusalem? Had he not foreseen a new heaven and a new earth, where death, pain and sorrow would be forever banished as man dwelt in perfect harmony with his Creator?

Our religious heritage was not only orthodox, but Calvinistic, with a heavy emphasis on individualism. Rejecting the sacerdotal authority of the Roman Catholic Church, it placed the ultimate responsibility for faith in the individual who stood alone before God. No church could speak or act in his behalf in passing the keys of the Kingdom. God and the individual had a direct relationship, of which God was the sole and final judge. Thus, although Calvinistic thought placed great emphasis on demonstrating by good works the fact of one's relationship to God, there could be no definitive

* See Quie, pp. 134–37.

outward test of inner faith. The Calvinist did not see his obligation in terms of either service in the social sector or obedience to the institutional church. He believed that in the last analysis he was responsible to God alone, for it was God alone, in the person of his son Jesus Christ, who served as the agent of grace and redemption.

Even more important was the Calvinist emphasis on God's providence. The *status quo* could always be rationalized since God was in his heaven and the earth was subject to his guiding control. Sometimes the opposite conclusion was drawn: as providence was clearly on the side of the church, churchmen accordingly appointed themselves as spokesmen for God in solving public issues. Thus in England the Republican revolution was partly led by Calvinist preachers who identified their political biases with their religious convictions.

However, before we too readily condemn this quasi-deterministic point of view, let us remember that twentieth-century man has often simply substituted his own different explanations for the older Calvinist doctrine. Marxism, psychologism, scientism, and political ideologies like liberalism and conservatism—each offers an explanation for the current state of affairs which can be used to support or discourage our attempts to intervene and bring about change in the social order.

Finally, we have said that the American religious heritage was evangelical. It stressed the personal involvement of the laity in spreading the message of the Gospel and carrying out the mission of the church. Social concern was minimized within the church; group relations and group obligations were not considered as important as individual spiritual ministries. Thus the foundation for Christian ethics and morality was essentially a personal one. This led to the view that human institutions and group relations could not be changed by restructuring them, but only by effecting a change of heart in the individuals who composed the groups or controlled the institutions.

In the parable of the seeds as it is told in the Gospel according to Saint Matthew, Christ taught that the Kingdom of Heaven could be likened to a field in which the owner had sown good seed, but his enemy under cover of darkness had come in and sown weeds. When his servants informed him, the owner suggested that they permit the tares to grow side by side with the good seed until the harvest, when the reapers would gather the weeds separately and bind them in bundles to be burned. When the disciples asked what the parable meant, Christ told them that the field was the world, the good seed the sons of the Kingdom, and the tares the sons of evil. The harvest represented the coming end of the age, when "the Son of Man will send his angels, and they will gather out of his kingdom all causes of sin and all evildoers, and throw them into the furnace of fire" (Matthew 13:41–42, RSV).

This parable and others like it have been used to support the view that nothing can really be done to counter institutionalized injustice and corruption in human society. Evangelicals have tended to feel that these corrupt institutions are merely a reflection of the sins of the world, which are to be dealt with in the final instance by God himself, when he pronounces judgment on us all at the end of the age. Therefore while Evangelicals have felt a responsibility to minister to the souls of men, they have often admitted to a fatalistic view that for the present age evil will flourish, and corporate society will necessarily embrace that evil. It would be going too far to suggest that Evangelicals have adopted a laissez-faire attitude toward political and socioeconomic issues, and yet events seem to have conspired to reduce the impact of evangelical thinking on these issues. For as modern society has become more and more highly organized, and as the individual has seen his own identity more and more submerged in the larger groups to which he belongs, the highly individualistic ethic of the Evangelical has come to seem less and less relevant. It is true that one of the most respected Evangelicals of our day, Billy Graham, apparently enjoys the role of confidant and friend to President Richard Nixon, as he did with former President Lyndon Johnson. But aside from a single appearance on Capitol Hill in support of antipoverty legislation, there is no evidence that he has consciously sought to influence the passage of particular legislation designed to meet particular social needs. There seems little likelihood that he will become the Protestant Cardinal Richelieu of the Nixon Administration despite his personal friendship with the President.

Thus orthodoxy, Calvinism, and evangelicalism combined to provide a theological basis for a social philosophy which stressed (1) limiting the purposes and powers of the state, (2) tempering the urgency of social issues with a belief in divine providence, and (3) treating social issues as the outgrowth of individual needs and conflicts.

These intellectual tendencies were reinforced by the prevailing economic conditions of the day. Colonial America was a largely rural society based on agriculture and cottage industries. Up until the end of the nineteenth century, the interior of the United States was a vast, often uncharted land where, with only a modicum of initiative, any man could find his place in the sun and stake his claim by dint of his own work. A farmer who needed more income could simply till more acreage, or move on to greener fields or more lucrative employment. The economic organization of our society was relatively simple, providing for ease of movement between jobs, places and firms. Our industries were smaller and more competitive, and thus more susceptible to being influenced by local conditions and by individuals. Life in a factory town could be transformed by sources of wealth within the community. Leading citizens traditionally fostered benevolence toward the poor of the community—an American version of *noblesse oblige.* And churches often collected food to feed the poor at the church door. Indeed, many Protestant churches still follow the practice of a retreat offering for the poor in conjunction with the communion service on the first Sunday of the month. The money from this offering is entrusted to the deacons who minister to the poor in the congregation or parish. (This tradition can be traced to the early church. On one of his journeys the Apostle Paul brought contributions from Macedonia and Achaia to the poor in the church at Jerusalem—Romans 15:26.)

But as the economic climate changed, individual initiative and response to social problems proved inadequate to the challenges of the new order. Improved communications and transportation facilities made people increasingly interdependent. The land supply ceased to be unlimited, so that men could no longer simply move west to start again. With the spread of large-scale industry, work became more technical and specialized; workers found themselves tied by training to a particular trade or job which they could no longer leave at will. And the unscrupulous entrepreneur's ability to exploit his labor sources expanded as the worker's ability to protect his own interests diminished. Likewise, individual Christians and individual congregations could no longer cope so easily with these problems, for the influence of the corporate institutions which were coming to dominate our economy was far greater than the influence of a local congregation.

Leaders in the church began to realize that an individualistic social ethic, based on personal outreach and wedded to the notion that social problems were not the business of the church, was simply inadequate to the problems of an emerging industrial society. They began to agitate, and to enlist the churches in a campaign for more vigorous policies in the public sector and more direction from the central government to cure social and economic injustices. This attempt to rearticulate the Christian social ethic in response to changing social conditions became known as the Social Gospel.

Had the Social Gospel leaders limited their efforts to sensitizing the church to the pressing social problems of industrialization, urbanization, and economic centralization, the ranks of American Protestants might not be as deeply split as they are today. But the Social Gospel movement eventually became much more than an attempt to restate Christian social imperatives and make the church relevant to the needs of modern society. It developed into an attack on religious orthodoxy itself. Leaders of the Social Gospel movement took up the claim that modern science had destroyed the basis for traditional interpretations of the authority of Scripture, thus challenging the cornerstone of Christian orthodoxy.

Those who clung to orthodox theology reacted sharply, charging that the leaders of the Social Gospel movement were not simply *relating* Christianity to the modern era, but *compromising* fundamental tenets of the New Testament faith. Thus what began as a movement to reevaluate the social ethic of the Christian message in light of contemporary problems had turned into a full-scale debate on the essence of Christianity itself. While orthodox thinkers looked to a future transcendent Kingdom of God, Social Gospel leaders spoke of transforming human society into a Kingdom of God of the here and now. Where orthodox thinkers stressed the divinity of Christ, their counterparts in the Social Gospel movement stressed his humanity.

Reacting against the Social Gospel, orthodox theologians reasserted what they considered to be the historic fundamentals of Christian teaching—hence they came to be known as Fundamentalists. Seen in this light, fundamentalism was a defense of orthodox Christianity in the face of the theological threat posed by the Social Gospel. But in the process of reacting against the *theology* of the Social Gospel, Fundamentalists also began to react against the *social* concerns which the leaders of this new school of theology were raising. A sort of guilt by association set in: social reformers were assumed to be theological liberals, and theological conservatives were expected to regard social questions not only as secondary to the essential mission of the church but as irrelevant and distracting to true Christian concern for the souls of men.

In *The Fundamentals,** a collection of several score brief essays in defense of the Fundamentalist movement, not one of the essays deals with social questions directly. Thus a controversy which began over social questions turned in the end to a theological debate over the meaning and integrity of Christian dogma. I believe it is at this point that the conservative religious community fell back into a conservative political and social posture. It occurred mainly as a reaction to the theological excesses of the Social Gospel

* *The Fundamentals: A Testimony to the Truth,* 12 vols. (Chicago, Testimony Publishing Company, 1910–1915).

movement, and much of the present linkage between conservative theological and conservative political interests is due to this heritage of opposition to the theological liberals.

The second explanation I would offer for this relationship between conservative and liberal political and religious persuasions is that much of it is simply due to confusion over what the terms "liberal" and "conservative" actually mean. In the religious sense, we do not have too much difficulty establishing the meaning of the terms: a liberal is one who assigns relatively less importance to articles of dogma as central to the Christian faith, or who is more ready to abandon traditional dogmatic formulations in the face of changing conditions or modern scientific argumentation; a theological conservative, on the other hand, would insist that the traditional dogmas are an essential foundation for Christian faith. Faced with possible conflict between science and Scripture, he would rather stand in opposition to the findings of modern science than the canons of Biblical authority.

But in the political realm, it is much more difficult to define exactly what we mean by "liberal" and "conservative." It is not uncommon to find an article in which someone claims that today's liberals are actually conservatives, and vice versa. Likewise, there is a tendency in America to use the terms in derogation rather than in description, thereby destroying some of their value for meaningful political discussion; or as someone has put it, "Labels become libels." Still, we must briefly discuss the meaning of these terms if we are to understand the problem we are examining.

Politically, the terms "liberal" and "conservative" are used in at least three ways. The most general is the easiest to understand: when we use the terms in a descriptive way to suggest that a liberal is for change, and a conservative against change. In this sense, it would be hard to label any Christian liberal or conservative on an *ipso facto* basis. As Reinhold Niebuhr points out, a Christian is both a liberal and a conservative, while at the same time being neither: he is a liberal insofar as he is called to be the salt of the earth, and insofar as his Christian calling sets him in constant opposition to the imperfect *status quo*—but he is a conservative insofar as he also knows that, so long as man is a sinner, mere social reform will never solve all of the problems that plague him in organized society. We are, to paraphrase Niebuhr, seeking proximate answers to insoluble problems. Thus there is no reason for a Christian to think of himself automatically as either a liberal or a conservative. His faith puts him in the position of being able to bridge the liberal-conservative dichotomy. The cynic might say that he thus enjoys the best of both worlds, but I believe it would be more accurate to say that this position gives a thinking Christian the responsibility of considering important issues from both points of view.

A second and more fruitful way of defining "liberal" and "conservative" is to recognize them as generic terms which became current in the seventeenth and eighteenth centuries during an extended debate over the nature of man in society. The liberals, including such writers as John Locke in England, Jean-Jacques Rousseau in France, and Tom Paine in America, held that man is an autonomous, rational creature who governs his personal and social life according to the dictates of reason. Social institutions are formed from rationally derived social contracts in which individuals agree that their interests are best secured by limiting government authority; in other words, that government is best which governs least. The original liberals were laissez-faire in their economic philosophy, and their model man might have been Robinson Crusoe. They regarded man's nature as essentially good. (Perhaps there were no uniform crime statistics to trouble them in those days.) They believed that social problems could be solved by revamping institutions in a manner which would allow each individual to reach his own state of perfection.

While these liberals may have been overly optimistic about the nature of man, and may have assigned too much importance to institutional reforms as a means of achieving social justice, they did leave behind a very important political heritage. For it was the first liberals, and not the conservatives, who originally developed the concept of constitutional limitations on government, in addition to the traditional liberal emphases on the rights of free speech and press and belief in the human dignity and moral worth of the individual.

In opposition to the liberals were the conservatives, typified by the great eighteenth-century English parliamentarian Edmund Burke. Horrified by the bloody excesses of the French Revolution which had been carried out in the name of reason and individual liberty, the conservatives held that man was much more (or perhaps much less) than a rational individual responsible to himself alone. He was a social being, with obligations to those around him, to the past, and to the future. Whereas the liberals acknowledged no authority in government except that which had been expressly granted in the social contract, the conservatives, scorning the idea of the innate goodness of man, maintained that as corruptible social beings men must be held in check by a due respect for the weight of tradition and law. Where Paine spoke of achieving justice, Burke was concerned to protect property—and of course these issues are still central to the debate between modern liberals and conservatives. Finally, the original conservatives argued that because man is a creature of passion as well as reason, politics involves considerably more than the adjustment of social institutions to meet rationally derived wants and needs—it is an art which must play as well to the passions of men who often behave with astounding irrationality despite their reluctance to acknowledge the fact.

Again, using this second set of meanings, we find that a Christian need not consider himself *ipso facto* a liberal or a conservative. Certainly the liberal emphasis on the dignity of the individual, and hence the rationale for limiting the power of government, are in accord with Christian teaching about the value of each child of God. The Old Testament clearly teaches that God sculpted man in his own image; Genesis 1:27 says, "So God created man in his own image, in the image of God created he him; male and female created he them" (KJV). Again in New Testament doctrine the divine Christ was also the Son of Man. The essence of his teaching was that each of us is precious in the sight of God.

At the same time, the liberal faith in the perfectibility of man through reason, education, and the manipulation of social institutions comes into conflict with Christian teaching about the sinful nature of fallen man. John the Apostle was making no exceptions when he said, "If we say we have no sin, we deceive ourselves, and the truth is not in us" (I John 1:8, RSV). Christ himself pointed up man's inability to reach perfection in his encounter with the rich young ruler, the prototype of all who seek earthly perfection. For despite his knowledge and observance of the law, this young man went away sorrowing because he could not bring himself to do the one thing that would have rendered his life perfect in the Master's eyes. Later on in this same passage, when the disciples expressed their fears that no man could qualify to enter the Kingdom of God, Christ answered them simply by saying, "With men this is impossible, but with God all things are possible" (Matthew 19:26, RSV).

The liberals also tell us that the state is nothing more than a social contract between consenting individuals seeking to achieve their own individual ends. The Bible, however, instructs us that the state is ordained of God as an instrument of his purpose on earth. The Apostle Paul makes this abundantly plain in the thirteenth chapter of Romans, when he declares: "For there is no authority except from God, and those that exist have been instituted by God" (Romans 13:1, RSV).

Insofar as the heritage of conservative thought is concerned, there is certainly much in common between Christian teaching about the state and the more organic view of society offered by the early conservative thinkers. Likewise, the conservative belief that man is not merely a creature of abstract reason, but of passion as well, is more in keeping with the concept of man as sinner.

On the other hand, the conservative viewpoint often fails to do justice to the Biblical idea of the absolute worth of the individual, apart from society as a whole or any social institution. Generally speaking, conservatives have not been in the vanguard of the civil-rights movement which gathered such force in the decade of the 1960's. Yet the essential worth of every human being—regardless of social status, education, lineage, or any other aspect of his existence—is really what the civil-rights movement is all about. It would seem that many conservative Christians have completely failed to appropriate for themselves the great doctrinal truth that they espouse to others—that all men are created of one blood and that God is no respecter of persons. They teach their children to sing, "Jesus loves

the little children, all the children of the world: red and
yellow, black and white, all are precious in his sight. . . ."
Yet in their mind's eye all these non-Caucasians are somehow located on the other side of the globe, where they
represent the exclusive concern of foreign missionaries.

To be sure, conservative Christians have always been
generous in their financial support of these efforts to save
the souls and heal the sick bodies of black, yellow and
brown people in foreign countries. Indeed, I suspect that
on a per-capita basis the giving in support of foreign mis-
sions is considerably higher in congregations where a conservative theology is preached from Sunday to Sunday than
it is in so-called liberal congregations. But sadly, I sometimes wonder if this form of generosity is not what C. S.
Lewis had in mind when he spoke of thrusting some particular responsibility to the very outer circumference of our
being so that we can continue to feel safe and secure at the
center of our being. I submit that those of us who really
cherish a belief that every person is precious in God's sight
have an obligation to honor that precept above all in those
familiar relationships that form the major part of our daily
lives.

There is a third set of meanings attached to the terms
"liberal" and "conservative" in contemporary American political usage. They are used to describe the ideologies of
our political leaders since the Roosevelt era. Whether we
agree with all of his policies or not, we must admit that
Franklin D. Roosevelt was one of our most dynamic and
forceful Presidents, and one of the most successful in ac-
complishing his political program and leaving his imprint
on the political structure of the United States. What Roosevelt did was to join some of the concepts of traditional
liberalism and conservatism in a new brand of liberalism.
And ever since his administration, these terms have more

and more been used in what we might call a post-Roosevelt sense.

The New Deal theorists argued that the ends of seventeenth-century liberalism could no longer be achieved through limited government, as the original liberals had contended. Rather, government itself would have to take an active role in providing for and protecting the individual. Where the seventeenth-century liberal had been concerned to protect his rights *against* the government, the New Deal liberal sought to achieve his rights *through* the government. Thus the New Deal era saw active intervention by the central government in areas which had traditionally been left to the natural laws of economics. The Federal government also became active in welfare and social legislation where heretofore incentives to individual initiatives had been considered an adequate response. The Roosevelt liberals adopted social concerns which had originally belonged to the conservatives, who had argued that individual rights and freedoms could only be measured in relation to their effect on society as a whole.

Though the New Deal liberals modified the classic liberalism of the seventeenth century by taking portions of eighteenth-century conservatism into their own creed, they retained their insistence on the goodness and perfectibility of man. Many seemed to believe that by reforming social institutions they could actually change man's nature for the better. They subscribed to the notion of inevitable human progress, and they claimed to have discovered (or to be in the process of discovering) scientific laws of government and social improvement.

Hard on the heels of the New Deal liberalism came a resurgence of classical conservatism, combined with a general reaction against the sweep and speed of the social changes brought about by the Roosevelt administration.

Thus the *status quo* type of conservative whom we originally discussed joined forces with the heirs of the original philosophical conservatives. These modern conservatives are a blend of (a) those who have reservations about the perfectibility of man and the unchecked use of government institutions for social reform, and (b) those who oppose the New Deal brand of liberalism out of political or financial self-interest. Many evangelical Christians seem to have a moral blind spot—or perhaps it is simply political naïveté—that prevents them from perceiving this seemingly obvious fact. There are a great many examples which could be cited: the Texas oil millionaire who believes that the depletion allowance is a sacrosanct tenet of political faith is not particularly interested in economic philosophy, but he is mighty interested in how this particular item will affect his profit-and-loss statement.

Here again, it is not possible to label either type of liberalism or conservatism as being particularly Christian. Certainly the sense of social justice which pervades New Deal liberalism is praiseworthy, but can the Christian fully accept belief in the perfectibility of man through social institutions or the evolutionary hypothesis often associated with the liberal movement? By the same token, the lack of social concern in certain sections of the modern conservative community is completely out of keeping with Biblical expressions of concern and love for our fellowman. Although I cannot vouch for the complete authenticity of the following statistic, it does illustrate the widening gap between social needs and our capacity to meet them: it is said that if every Protestant church family were so poor as to be on welfare, and yet paid a tithe of its meager income to the church, the total sum thus made available would exceed the present income of all Protestant churches in America by some 35 percent.

But is there not something to be said for the modern conservative's distrust of turning to government for all our needs at the expense of individual prerogatives? Does not the integrity of the individual stand threatened? Note that here we have a strange reversal: the New Deal liberal is really closer to the eighteenth-century conservative, with his organic view of the state in which individual liberties must sometimes be curbed in the interests of society as a whole; and the modern conservative shares the seventeenth-century liberal's concern for the integrity of the individual and his distrust of governmental power.

Hence, in talking about political liberals and conservatives, we must first define our terms very carefully. For today's liberal may well be yesterday's conservative, and vice versa, depending on what set of meanings we attach to the terms. The ambiguity of these terms is one reason (not the only one, of course) why a growing number of politicians carefully eschew the use of either label. They prefer to be called moderates, an equally ambivalent term, to be sure, but far less susceptible to damaging misconstructions. Finally, we must also recognize—as I have tried to point out briefly along the way—that in no case do we find that one position or the other has a monopoly on Christian truth and understanding vis-à-vis social problems and their solutions.

The third basic proposition I would like to offer about the contemporary linkage between conservative and liberal political and religious persuasions follows from the points we have made earlier. As this phenomenon is partly a result of the historic tension between the Social Gospel movement and resurgent fundamentalism, and partly a result of confusion over what the terms "liberal" and "conservative"

actually mean today, it seems to me that there are both rational and irrational grounds for this alignment. In other words, while there are certain dogmatic and ideological points of affinity between religious and political conservatism on the one hand and their liberal counterparts on the other, some of the other important ties that bind these communities together (unofficially to be sure) are arbitrary and to that extent emotional rather than rational.

What are the rational grounds on which a religious conservative might be expected to adopt a conservative political viewpoint, and vice versa?

First, conservative theology insists that man is a fallen creature, inescapably tainted by sin and sanctified only through the power of God. Bluntly put, this doctrine severely limits what hope we may have for "improving" the human race through education and environmental reform. The conservative cannot completely accept the faith in man's ability to learn which is implicit in H. G. Wells's famous dictum: "Human history becomes more and more a race between education and catastrophe."

Liberal theology is more comfortable with Wells's point of view, and therefore it can place its hope in the reform of political institutions, the feeding of the poor, the education of the illiterate, the enfranchisement of the disenfranchised, the improvement of labor conditions, etc. At the same time, we should be careful to point out that the optimism of many liberals has been noticeably dampened by two world wars, which saw the mass bombing of civilians, the use of poison gases and the slaughter of six million Jews; the cold war which followed, featuring brutalities in Communist states around the world and increasingly rigid propaganda postures on both sides; and finally the failure of some of the liberals' most highly vaunted domestic programs, such as welfare, job creation and civil-rights legislation, to solve our most pressing problems at home. Where once they sang, "Every day in every way, man is getting better and better," many liberals today are more willing to question their philosophical premises, although they have been slow to produce new ones to justify their political activism. Daniel Moynihan, President Nixon's adviser on domestic programs, has noted wryly that the central government has proved to be much more effective at collecting money than dispensing it.

Secondly, conservative theology holds that the Kingdom of God is a transcendent, other-worldly Kingdom. Therefore none of our programs—be they governmental, private, international, or what not—should ever be viewed as divinely given panaceas for human problems. Conservatives cannot place their faith in a New Deal, a Fair Deal, a New Frontier, a Great Society, or even a New Federalism. They insist that there are two cities to which man owes his allegiance—and only the City of God will be able to offer perfect social justice. The League of Nations, the United Nations, a superior defense system, a healthy international economy—none of these will bring final and lasting peace, for none of them address themselves to the basic sinfulness of man.

We might well point out in this connection that conservative theology is often no more consistent than liberal theology when it enters the political arena. The same conservative theologians who look askance at expenditures for domestic social programs have not always been as critical or as vocal in protesting huge expenditures on armaments. It is not that they have a special place in their hearts for the munitions makers and the merchants of death. Rather they more readily assume that the sky-rocketing military budget—which has jumped from $50 billion under President Eisenhower to $80 billion under President Nixon—is a necessary and logical outgrowth of the powers of general government.

But while there is much in conservative theology which runs counter to doctrinaire political liberalism, it also includes elements which might open the door to a practical liberalism. Many of the concerns of the New Deal were and continue to be not just liberal causes as such, but right in themselves. Minimum standards of health, food and shelter, for example, need not be considered simply as problems of charity or benevolence; they are basic human rights. A legal guarantee of civil rights for all Americans regardless of race or color may not put an end to hatred and distrust between black and white—we may not be able to legislate love between different colored children of God —but certainly civil rights ought not to be denied any man because of his race, for equality before the law is a right deriving from the fact of humanity. Was the divine breath of life that made man a living soul either black or white, yellow or brown?

Many of today's theological conservatives are still debating the tired old questions raised by the Social Gospel. Instead of facing current political issues squarely, they strike at the straw ghosts of an era long gone. Likewise, many theological liberals today have failed to consider adequately the impact of sin on the individual and his community, and thus have failed to recognize that institutional reform, no matter how well-intentioned or how sweeping, can never make human society any better collectively than it is individually.

I spoke earlier of a growing tendency for politicians to seek the label of "moderate." I believe we need more spiritual moderates. This does not in my view involve any compromise of basic Scriptural truths, but it may require some to cast off the entirely man-made prejudices with which those basic truths have become encrusted. As Christians we must learn to transcend both political conservatism and political liberalism, and to weigh the claims of both in terms of our Christian faith. This will not necessarily lead to agreement among Christians on political issues—for Christians no less than others are subject to self-interest and self-protection in their evaluation of political priorities —but it ought to lead to a new awareness of the energy and inspiration that Christians *as Christians* can bring to politics, which is nothing more or less than our collective attempt to solve our current social problems. Christians ought to have a unique vantage point from which to consider these problems, and a unique contribution to make in helping to solve them.

In reporting on a conference on the environment recently held in Alaska, *The New York Times* wrote that some of the participants cited our Judeo-Christian heritage as one reason for the present environmental crisis. The reasoning went something like this: the Bible teaches that God created our planet for man's use and enjoyment; since then we have used the divine mandate to subdue the earth and exercise dominion over it, but in the process we have polluted our streams, poisoned the very air that we breathe, and so defiled our human habitat that our future existence is in jeopardy.

However, this interpretation leaves out some very important elements of the story of Creation. God also told man to "be fruitful and multiply, and replenish the earth" (Genesis 1:28, KJV). It ignores as well the fact that "God saw everything that he had made, and behold, it was very good" (Genesis 1:31, RSV). If we have despoiled our environment and plundered the resources that were divinely wrought, it is in disobedience rather than in fulfillment of God's plan for the universe which he created. God placed man in the garden which he had planted eastward in Eden. That garden has become perverted into something very unlovely—into the asphalt jungle of the city ghetto and the scarred and ravaged rural landscape where the apocalyptic forces of hunger, poverty and disease stalk their prey.

The crisis we face today is a crisis of the spiritual environment as well as the physical one. In times past, when our nation has faced impending danger, we have managed to subordinate if not eliminate our differences as we rallied our resources to meet the common foe. Today we need committed Christian citizens who are willing to overlook doctrinal and ideological differences in order to make common cause against the forces that otherwise threaten to overwhelm us. If we do not, we will be forced to admit to that gloomy assessment of the world once voiced by the Irish poet W. B. Yeats:*

> Things fall apart, the center cannot hold;
> Mere anarchy is loosed upon the world.
> The blood-dimmed tide is loosed, and everywhere
> The ceremony of innocence is drowned;
> The best lack all conviction, while the worst
> Are full of passionate intensity.

Today there are Christians of both conservative and liberal persuasion who would substitute political unity for spiritual unity as the sign of a socially concerned and effective church. But surely this is a distortion of the church's mission. Christians may disagree on specific policy questions, and yet still infuse the entire political system with energy, direction and commitment of immeasurable value.

We do not need conservative Christians who will become

* Reprinted with permission of The Macmillan Company, Mr. M. B. Yeats, and Macmillan & Co. from *Collected Poems* by William Butler Yeats. Copyright 1924 by The Macmillan Company, renewed 1952 by Bertha Georgia Yeats.

liberal political activists, or vice versa. What we do desperately need is Christians who will begin to consider seriously each political issue on its merits in the light of their religious convictions. We must stop using religion as an implicit justification for our political biases, and learn instead to give our faith new expression in our politics.

APPENDIX I

The following is the text of the Code of Official Conduct adopted by the U.S. Senate in 1968:

Resolved, It is declared to be the policy of the Senate that—

(a) The ideal concept of public office, expressed by the words, "A public office is a public trust," signifies that the officer holds this power in trust to be used only for their benefit and never for the benefit of himself or of a few; and that the officer must never conduct his own affairs so as to infringe on the public interest. All official conduct of Members of the Senate should be guided by this paramount concept of public office.

(b) These rules, as the written expression of certain standards of conduct, complement the body of unwritten but generally accepted standards that continue to apply to the Senate.

SEC. 2. The Standing Rules of the Senate are amended by adding at the end thereof the following new rules:

"RULE XLI
"Outside Business or Professional Activity or Employment by Officers or Employees

"1. No officer or employee whose salary is paid by the Senate may engage in any business or professional activity or employment for compensation unless—

"(a) the activity or employment is not inconsistent nor in conflict with the conscientious performance of his official duties; and

"(b) he has reported in writing when this rule takes effect or when his office or employment starts and on the 15th day of May in each year thereafter the nature of any personal service, activity or employment to his supervisor. The supervisor shall then, in the discharge of his duties, take such action as he considers necessary for the avoidance of conflict of interest or interference with duties to the Senate.

"2. For the purpose of this rule—

"(a) a Senator or the Vice President is the supervisor of his administrative, clerical, or other assistants;

"(b) a Senator who is the chairman of a committee is the supervisor of the professional, clerical, or other assistants to the committee except that minority staff members shall be under the supervision of the ranking minority Senator on the committee;

"(c) a Senator who is a chairman of a subcommittee which has its own staff and financial authorization is the supervisor of the professional, clerical, or other assistants to the subcommittee except that minority staff members shall be under the supervision of the ranking minority Senator on the subcommittee;

"(d) the President pro tem is the supervisor of the Secretary of the Senate, Sergeant at Arms and Doorkeeper, the Chaplain, and the employees of the Office of the Legislative Counsel;

"(e) the Secretary of the Senate is the supervisor of the employees of his office;

"(f) the Sergeant at Arms and Doorkeeper is the supervisor of the employees of his office;

"(g) the Majority and Minority Leaders and the Majority and Minority Whips are the supervisors of the research, clerical, or other assistants assigned to their respective offices;

"(h) the Majority Leader is the supervisor of the Secretary

for the Majority. The Secretary for the Majority is the supervisor of the employees of his office; and

"(i) the Minority Leader is the supervisor of the Secretary for the Minority. The Secretary for the Minority is the supervisor of the employees of his office.

"3. This rule shall take effect ninety days after adoption.

"RULE XLII
"CONTRIBUTIONS

"1. A Senator or person who has declared or otherwise made known his intention to seek nomination or election, or who has filed papers or petitions for nomination or election, or on whose behalf a declaration or nominating paper or petition has been made or filed, or who has otherwise, directly or indirectly, manifested his intention to seek nomination or election, pursuant to State law, to the office of United States Senator, may accept a contribution from—

"(a) a fund-raising event organized and held primarily in his behalf, provided—

"(1) he has expressly given his approval of the fund-raising event to the sponsors before any funds were raised; and

"(2) he receives a complete and accurate accounting of the source, amounts, and disposition of the funds raised; or

"(b) an individual or an organization, provided the Senator makes a complete and accurate accounting of the source, amount, and disposition of the funds received; or

"(c) his political party when such contributions were from a fund-raising event sponsored by his party, without giving his express approval for such fund-raising event when such fund-raising event is for the purpose of providing contributions for candidates of his party and such contributions are reported by the Senator or candidate as provided in paragraph (b).

"2. The Senator may use the contribution only to influence his nomination for election, or his election, and shall not use, directly or indirectly, any part of any contribution for any other purpose, except as otherwise provided herein.

"3. Nothing in this rule shall preclude the use of contributions to defray expenses for travel to and from each Senator's home State; for printing and other expenses in connection with the mailing of speeches, newsletters, and reports to a Senator's constituents; for expenses of radio, television, and news media methods of reporting to a Senator's constituents; for telephone, telegraph, postage, and stationery expenses in excess of allowance; and for newspaper subscriptions from his home State.

"4. All gifts in the aggregate amount or value of $50 or more received by a Senator from any single source during a year, except a gift from his spouse, child, or parent, and except a contribution under sections 1 and 2, shall be reported under rule XLIV.

"5. This rule shall take effect ninety days after adoption.

"RULE XLIII
"POLITICAL FUND ACTIVITY BY
OFFICERS AND EMPLOYEES

"1. No officer or employee whose salary is paid by the Senate may receive, solicit, be the custodian of, or distribute any funds in connection with any campaign for the nomination for election, or the election of any individual to be a Member of the Senate or to any other Federal office. This prohibition does not apply to any assistant to a Senator who has been designated by that Senator to perform any of the functions described in the first sentence of this paragraph and who is compensated at a rate in excess of $10,000 per annum if such designation has been made in writing and filed with the Secretary of the Senate. The Secretary of the Senate shall make the designation available for public inspection.

"2. This rule shall take effect sixty days after adoption.

"RULE XLIV
"Disclosure of Financial Interests

"1. Each Senator or person who has declared or otherwise made known his intention to seek nomination or election, or who has filed papers or petitions for nomination or election, or on whose behalf a declaration or nominating paper or petition has been made or filed, or who has otherwise, directly or indirectly, manifested his intention to seek nomination or election, pursuant to State law, to the office of United States Senator, and each officer or employee of the Senate who is compensated at a rate in excess of $15,000 a year, shall file with the Comptroller General of the United States, in a sealed envelope marked 'Confidential Personal Financial Disclosure of ――――,' before (name) the 15th day of May in each year, the following reports of his personal financial interests:

"(a) a copy of the returns of taxes, declaration, statements, or other documents which he, or he and his spouse jointly, made for the preceding year in compliance with the income tax provisions of the Internal Revenue Code;

"(b) the amount or value and source of each fee or compensation of $1,000 or more received by him during the preceding year from a client; and

"(c) the name and address of each business or professional corporation, firm, or enterprise in which he was an officer, director, partner, proprietor, or employee who received compensation during the preceding year and the amount of such compensation;

"(d) the identity of each interest in real or personal property having a value of $10,000 or more which he owned at any time during the preceding year;

"(e) the identity of each trust or other fiduciary relation in which he held a beneficial interest having a value of $10,000 or more, and the identity if known of each interest of the trust or other fiduciary relation in real or personal property in which the Senator, officer, or employee held a beneficial interest having a value of $10,000 or more, at any time during the preceding year. If he cannot obtain the identity of the fiduciary interests, the Senator, officer, or employee shall request the fiduciary to report that information to the Comptroller General in the same manner that reports are filed under this rule;

"(f) the identity of each liability of $5,000 or more owned by him, or by him and his spouse jointly, at any time during the preceding year; and

"(g) the source and value of all gifts in the aggregate amount or value of $50 or more from any single source received by him during the preceding year.

"2. Except as otherwise provided by this section, all papers filed under section 1 of this rule shall be kept by the Comptroller General for not less than seven years, and while so kept shall remain sealed. Upon receipt of a resolution of the Select Committee on Standards and Conduct, adopted by a recorded majority vote of the full committee, requesting the transmission to the committee of any of the reports filed by any individual under section 1 of this rule, the Comptroller General shall transmit to the committee the envelopes containing such reports. Within a reasonable time after such recorded vote has been taken, the individual concerned shall be informed of the vote to examine and audit, and shall be advised of the nature and scope of such examination. When any sealed envelope containing any such report is received by the committee, such envelope may be opened and the contents thereof may be examined only by members of the committee in executive session. If, upon such examination, the committee determines that further consideration by the committee is warranted and is within the jurisdiction of the committee, it may make the contents of any such envelope available for any use by any member of the committee, or any member of the staff of the committee, which is required for the discharge of his official duties. The committee may receive the papers as evidence, after giving to the individual concerned due notice and opportunity for hearing in a closed session. The Comptroller General shall report to the Select Committee on Standards and Conduct not later than the 1st day of June in each year the names of Senators, officers and employees who have filed a report. Any paper which has been filed with the Comptroller General for longer than seven years, in accordance with the provisions of this section, shall be returned to the individual concerned or his legal representative. In the event of the death or termination of service of a Member of the Senate, an officer or employee, such papers shall be returned unopened to such individual, or to the surviving spouse or legal representative of such individual within one year of such death or termination of service.

"3. Each Senator or person who has declared or otherwise made known his intention to seek nomination or election, or who has filed papers or petitions for nomination or election, or on whose behalf a declaration or nominating paper or petition has been made or filed, or who has otherwise, directly or indirectly, manifested his intention to seek nomination or election, pursuant to State law, to the office of United States Senator, and each officer or employee of the Senate who is compensated at a rate in excess of $15,000 a year, shall file with the Secretary of the Senate, before the 15th day of May in each year, the following reports of his personal financial interests:

"(a) the accounting required by rule XLII for all contributions received by him during the preceding year, except that contributions in the aggregate amount or value of less than $50 received from any single source during the reporting period may be totaled without further itemization; and

"(b) the amount or value and source of each honorarium of $300 or more received by him during the preceding year.

"4. All papers filed under section 3 of this rule shall be kept by the Secretary of the Senate for not less than three years and shall be made available promptly for public inspection and copying.

"5. This rule shall take effect on July 1, 1968. No reports shall be filed for any period before office or employment was held with the Senate, or during a period of office or employment with the Senate of less than ninety days in a year; except that the Senator, or officer or employee of the Senate, may file a copy of the return of taxes for the year 1968, or a report of substantially equivalent information for only the effective part of the year 1968."

SEC. 3. It is the sense of the Senate that appropriate action to be taken with respect to the requirements imposed by this resolution upon Members and officers and employees of the Senate for the purpose of imposing uniform requirements upon all Members and officers and employees of the House of Representatives, all officers and employees of the executive branch of the Government, including members of the Armed Forces, and all officers and employees of the judicial branch of the Government.

APPENDIX II

The following is the text of the Code of Official Conduct adopted by the U.S. House of Representatives in 1968:

1. A Member, officer; or employee of the House of Representatives shall conduct himself at all times in a manner which shall reflect creditably on the House of Representatives.

2. A Member, officer, or employee of the House of Representatives shall adhere to the spirit and the letter of the Rules of the House of Representatives and to the rules of duly constituted committees thereof.

3. A Member, officer, or employee of the House of Representatives shall receive no compensation nor shall he permit any compensation to accrue to his beneficial interest from any source, the receipt of which would occur by virtue of influence improperly exerted from his position in the Congress.

4. A Member, officer, or employee of the House of Representatives shall accept no gift of substantial value, directly or indirectly, from any person, organization, or corporation having a direct interest in legislation before the Congress.

5. A Member, officer, or employee of the House of Representatives shall accept no honorarium for a speech, writing for publication, or other similar activity, from any person, organization, or corporation in excess of the usual and customary value for such services.

6. A member of the House of Representatives shall keep his campaign funds separate from his personal funds. He shall

convert no campaign funds to personal use in excess of reimbursement for legitimate and verifiable prior campaign expenditures. He shall expend no funds from his campaign account not attributable to bona fide campaign purposes.

7. A Member of the House of Representatives shall treat as campaign contributions all proceeds from testimonial dinners or other fund raising events if the sponsors of such affairs do not give clear notice in advance to the donors or participants that the proceeds are intended for other purposes.

8. A Member of the House of Representatives shall retain no one from his clerk hire allowance who does not perform duties commensurate with the compensation he receives.

As used in the Code of Official Conduct of the House of Representatives—

a) the terms "Member" and "Member of the House of Representatives" include the Resident Commissioner from Puerto Rico; and

b) the term "officer or employee of the House of Representatives" means any individual whose compensation is disbursed by the Clerk of the House of Representatives.